WELL DONE

WELL DONE

A WWII Memoir
From Childhood Dreams To Naval Aviator

Nancy Hungerford

Library of Congress Control Number: 2021901874
ISBN: Hardcover   978-1-6641-5486-5
                   Softcover   978-1-6641-5485-8
                   eBook   978-1-6641-5484-1

Print information available on the last page.

Rev. date: 02/17/2021

To order additional copies of this book, contact:
Xlibris
844-714-8691
www.Xlibris.com
Orders@Xlibris.com
801751

Author's Note

The author has relied on the logs and journals kept by her husband and members of his squadron during WW11 for this memoir. I have made every effort to check the accuracy of military events, names and dates. Should there be an error, I welcome receiving any corrections.

Robert, 1928
"Sailing…"

"Or flying?"

To all the WWII veterans, men and women, who courageously stood up and served their country by land, air, or sea.

To the women left at home who didn't hesitate to take up the void in the workforce while running their households and raising their children alone.

To all those who anxiously waited for mail when the censors wouldn't let servicemen write.

To the children born while their fathers were at war.

And to loved ones who prayed they would not and yet did receive the dreaded telegram or the knock on their door. "The Navy Department regrets to inform you . . ."

Contents

Acknowledgments

From Bob, November 2008

The contents of *Well Done* grew without intention. My observations were written in notebooks while aboard the USS *Franklin* in 1944—I also had my flying logs for reference. Memories floated to the top of my consciousness at random moments over sixty years, connected without a plan or plot. They were waiting to be developed into a memoir, which I simply never put down on the page.

Nancy, my wife, told me, "Organize your logs and diaries. We are going to write a book." Thanks to her, this project began.

Phil vanDusen, compatriot in the "Big Apple" advertising wars, jumped on the bandwagon. He encouraged and counseled—he became my cheerleader.

Teddy Thompson, a.k.a. Gambino, another "mad man," provided positive boosts, plus good laughs, adding his own razzle-dazzle.

Nothing would have been "Navy" without the enthusiastic input from my squadron buddies: Bill Dorie, Gene Higgins, Will Gove, and Allee Downs. They helped fill in events, facts, and squadron history of days long gone.

The official navy history of VF-13 (declassified) was made available by Johnny B. Johnson.

Jack Stilwill, a.k.a. Uncle Joe, loaned witty versions from his "squadron saga."

My martini pal, Carolyn Matalene, professor of English at the University of South Carolina and fellow Midwesterner, provided thoughtful suggestions.

From Nancy, November 2020

"The book" became a private family joke. Probably only the Bible took longer to write. For better or worse, here are friends who helped me fulfill this long effort—turning Bob's logs and journals into *Well Done*.

Charles Clayton dismissed many useless words, semicolons, and adjectives, taking me to another level.

Rick Constant, former Vietnam veteran, and John Holzapfel and Ted Web, pals from our Orient Yacht Club sailing days, added corrections I failed to see.

Helpful hands, too many to mention, assisted me with organizing what seemed to be overwhelming stacks of papers.

Chris Fouchet—love to you for patiently reading chapters to Bob, giving him the joy and self-esteem of participation.

Tom Combs's care of Bob kept me going during the hard final weeks and days. That in itself was a contribution to this book.

In the same way, Jim, Jenny, Connor, Meghan, Andrew—you gave uplifting smiles to me, more important to the "Great."

I thank all of you from the bottom of my heart for helping me write Bob's story, *Well Done*.

Prologue

I am on a Long Island ferry crossing the Sound, heading home after a visit in Connecticut. Despite the roar of the ferry engines, I opt to remain in our car, facing aft on the lower deck. My wife, Nancy, sits with our aging "Persian prince" cat snoozing on her lap while I decide to stretch my legs and walk the upper deck before the second phase of our trip.

I settle on a bench out of the prevailing wind and notice geese flying overhead in a perfect V formation, honking directions toward their way back to their summer nesting grounds. Clusters of shorebirds flying low above the water are following their migratory path. It's the signal of another summer ahead, all in perfect harmony.

Mesmerized by the steady flow of whitecaps rolling on the gray-green wash of the ferry's propellers, I realize I am–like the seasons–in the winter of my life. I drift back in time to my boyhood dreams of flying, which finally, through determination, turned into reality. I became a young navy fighter aviator aboard the USS *Franklin*, a carrier in the Pacific theater involved in some of the largest battles of World War II and victim of an epic kamikaze bombing.

Today is Memorial Day, which for most marks the start of summer fun. I wonder if the true meaning of this day, taking time to remember and honor all those who lost their lives while serving our country, becomes lost in this long weekend holiday. The small flags and hanging banners are not just fluttering frills to celebrate the beginning of summer. The colors at half-staff do not signal a reminder to shop for holiday bargains at the mall, nor is taps a signal to light the charcoal on the grill.

In 1866, this holiday began as Decoration Day, when grieving families who lost their sons and loved ones to the Civil War gathered to decorate their graves. It was to pay honor to those lost while the memories of that war were still freshly raw and painful. Does everyone realize that the bits of red paper formed into poppies resemble the real vibrant blossoms among the rows upon rows of crosses in Flanders and are in memory of yet another generation who died in the horrors of WWI? WWI was supposed to be "the war to end all wars," yet it seems we just can't get it right. Most towns have parades and lay wreaths, but do the young marchers realize that the freedoms they enjoy today were earned by men and women not much older than themselves whose memories we should hold sacred on this day?

I reflect on all this and then wonder how I reached ninety-one years of age—fortunate enough to experience marriage, children, weddings, funerals, and great-grandchildren and still be here. I don't think of my time as a Navy fighter aviator very often, but now and then during a solitary moment like this and because it is a day of remembering, my thoughts shift to war with all its senseless pain and suffering. I realize there were enemies of our country, enemies who were men I didn't see or know and killed without guilt, sorrow, or celebration—a personal terror I experienced that can never be explained or understood, not even by myself.

I was a naive young man with a childhood dream to become an aviator. The USS *Franklin* became my home, which formed my transition from an idealistic dreamer to a navy fighter aviator, burnished, hardened through pain, fear, and seeing death. The USS *Franklin* housed a large diverse community, a family that never failed to welcome the fighter pilots returning to the safety of its deck, our home.

I was young, somewhat of a romantic, I suppose. I thought I was invincible. At nineteen, I believed the *Franklin*—my home of steel—and I were indestructible. I had never heard the word *kamikaze*.

Introduction

It is 1944. I am aboard the USS *Franklin*, the aircraft carrier assigned to combat in the Pacific theater during World War II. I wait in anticipation with the other members of our squadron in the tension-filled ready room for our orders to come over the speaker.

Upon hearing the flight plan, all pilots walk calmly yet briskly to the deck toward our designated aircraft. Propellers are already whirling; plane and life jackets have been made ready for takeoff. Each plane is prepared, carrying a parachute, an automatic pistol, and a jungle survival kit, all of which we hope we will never have to use.

While the flight deck is massive, the space seems postage-stamp small, considering it must function as a takeoff and landing airstrip for the squadrons of Hellcats, dive-bombers, and torpedoes. What seems to be routine activity calls for tremendous skill and accuracy on the part of the Airedales or plane pushers, whose job consists in lining up the planes to ready for takeoff. Grumman Hellcats, the most important fighter planes of the war in the Pacific, were lined up first on the deck with the dive-bombers behind them. Behind the dive-bombers was the torpedo squadron.

My squadron, the Fighting Thirteen, leads the takeoff. Our assignment today is to prevent the enemy planes from getting through the protective screen of the carrier and to assure that the bomber squadron can safely begin their mission. I pay strict attention to the signalmen and move my plane into position for takeoff. I am alert, adrenaline rushing, feeling both calm and nervous. I'm in my plane, waiting for the signal for my turn to zoom off the deck on our designated mission. I have a few seconds to take a deep breath. My "lucky scary face" pin is pinned to the back of my helmet to scare away any "bad guys" who may try to sneak up on me from behind.

Our skipper, Bill Coleman, an Annapolis guy, is the first to take off. Next, his wingman takes off to position himself to the right of the skipper. The left lead follows and then his wingman. All pilots follow in the same order from right to left, each with a wingman in place, until all eight of the squadron are safely in the air. I am a Navy fighter aviator, and I say a quick prayer that God, fate, and luck will bring me back from this mission to the safety of the *Franklin*'s deck along with all my comrades in the Fighting Thirteen.

Part One

Before The War

Growing Up

- 1 -

I find it interesting to look back at our childhood and wonder which people and what events had the most influence on our lives and shaped our destiny. I was born on November 11, 1921, with the help of a midwife at our home in Detroit, Michigan, on a sheet- and blanket-covered dining room table. It was not unusual to be born at home at that time; many women preferred it to a hospital, attended to by a midwife who served as the delivery "doctor." "Get towels and boil some water" was not a joke line then. My mother, who had several previous miscarriages, had a long and difficult labor. Dad later joyfully wrote to relatives, "Our adorable chubby baby boy was born healthy, and my dear, dear Ellie is doing fine. My poor darling had such a hard time of it, having been in labor for several days, but now all is well. We couldn't be happier and can't wait for you to see him. We named him Robert Vernon Hungerford, Vernon from my middle name, and we liked the name Robert. Of course, we already call him Bobby."

My dad, who had studied tool and die making at night in trade school, was a foreman at the Kelsey-Hayes Wheel Factory. It was a good-paying and very secure job. Little did he know that, within eight years after my birth, he would be looking for all and any additional jobs he could find to support us when the Great Depression hit in 1929 and when masses of people were unemployed, had lost their entire savings, were jumping out of windows in desperation, and were standing on food lines for the first time in their lives.

Mom, who was a dedicated mother and homemaker, used her skillful housekeeping efforts during those depression years to help shield us from the worst economic woes of the period. Magically, she managed to make us feel as though nothing was lacking in our lives, although I walked to many destinations rather than using the car or public transportation. She and I would walk to church every Sunday, which was quite a distance away. I trudged through my own daily walk to school, which was close to a mile each way; rain, cold, or sleet was no excuse.

As a boy, at much too young an age, my dad had to become a part-time breadwinner to contribute to his family, which included his brothers, Willie, Charlie, and Harold. As a result, he was never able to finish school past the sixth grade. Like my dad, my mom was also deprived of finishing her education. Her father had a secure position at the Ford factory, but her mother had a rather serious heart condition. After completing the eighth grade, her presence was required at home to help her sickly mother with the care of her three younger siblings, Dolly, Katie, and Marvin. Sadly, she witnessed the death of her only brother, Marvin, when he was just eight. In those days, a common cold could easily turn into pneumonia, resulting in death within a few weeks.

When I look back at that time, I believe Mom and Dad made it through such a difficult period because they were very much in love. Later in life, when they were both gone, I found all the saved love notes and cards my dad sent to my mom for every occasion, with many for no occasion at all. I suppose one could call those written notes of his "just because." They were his romantic way of expressing his continued love and appreciation for her.

Each day just before Dad would come home from work, my mom would put on a fresh dress and primp and fix her hair with a final touch of fresh lipstick. I once asked her, "Where are you going, Mom?"

"Nowhere," she replied. "Dad is almost due home for dinner."

She added, "I always want to look special for him."

Given their hard efforts to get ahead and the sacrifices they had made, it wasn't surprising that higher education was a firm dictate to me from both my parents to improve my life and have less of a struggle than they had gone through. I, on the other hand—being an only child, more than likely spoiled, pampered, and totally unaware of the seriousness of life—found that studying and setting goals were not exactly my strong point. That would change.

"Bobby"

A door-to-door photographer with pony in tow took this photo.

Flying Daydreams

- 2 -

"Come on, Billy, let's bike to the airport."

Every summer I would spend a week or two with my mother's sister Aunt Dolly and her husband, Uncle Russel, along with their young son, David, in Grand Rapids, Michigan. My parents would drive me to their house, where I had my own summer bedroom. At the start of our trip, Dad would strap my green standard bike on top of our green Essex car so I'd have some summer transportation to get around. My standard bike didn't have fancy hand brakes, so you had to push reverse on the pedals to stop, and the speeds—well, that was up to you. The faster you pedaled, the faster it went.

Billy, who lived down the street, was my age, and we were the best of summer pals, each of us looking forward to our summer vacation and catching up while comparing all the school events we had gone through that year. Especially important, did we have a new girlfriend? We would hang out and ride around on our bikes, looking for something to do to pass the time. Billy was a good sport and always up for a new adventure, so it didn't take much persuasion for him to join me on my favorite bike ride of all. My destination was about five miles, all uphill from Aunt Dolly's house to a small local airport—well, if one could call it an airport. It consisted of one single open hangar and a large grass takeoff field.

Usually, if we were lucky, a few private single-wing planes might be there, but that didn't matter to me. It was an airport, and there would be at least one plane we could investigate. We would pretend the plane we were checking out was ours, and we'd talk about all the destinations beyond our bikes that we would travel to on our imaginary flights. I would be the pilot, and Billy would be the navigator.

I would run my hands over the canvas tail wings, peek in the window, and look at the two leather seats, the instruments, the control stick, the pedals to control the tail, and the fuel and speed gauges. I was fourteen, and hanging around the planes built up my romantic notion that I would one day become a pilot, not just any pilot but like one of those hero WWI ace pilots I read about. Their bravado during that war made them as famous as matadors, movie stars, or race car drivers. They were the out-of-the-ordinary personage who voluntarily put themselves in a fast, complex danger zone, the ultimate test represented by combat.

Back home, my best friend, Willis, and I would play cowboys and Indians, with Willis wearing his fake fur chaps and both of us sporting big hats along with our toy cap guns. We would have fun, but I never really wanted to be a cowboy with a big hat and smoking guns. I wanted to wear a smart uniform, like Errol Flynn, along with a white silk scarf, goggles, and a helmet while flying top speed in the air. No horses for me.

When my uncle Russel or my dad would fill up their cars, I always pleaded with them to head for a Shell gas station. Shell had a promotion at the time, and with each gas purchase, you received a poster depicting the latest aerobatic aircraft maneuvers. I kept those treasured posters hanging inside my bedroom closet door and studied the maneuvers along with their illustrated instructions. There were so many—the slow roll, the snap roll, the chandelle, the Cuban eight, and my favorite, the Immelmann turn. I suppose this was my favorite after reading about Max Immelmann, Germany's WWI ace pilot known as the Eagle of Lille.

After making an attack on an enemy aircraft, the trick to Immelmann's dogfight maneuver was his control of high speed, going into a roll and repositioning his plane for another surprise attack from above the enemy. He was the first ace pilot to be awarded the Blue Max medal. He was my hero. *Someday*, I thought, *I might be just like him.* I would memorize and practice each of those maneuvers to no end, if only in my mind and in the safety of my bedroom.

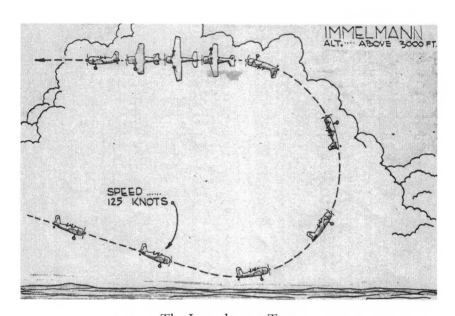

The Immelmann Turn

Charting A Course

- 3 -

Today entering college is a matter of test scores. Back then, the high school principal's recommendation counted. Mr. McNally, our principal, only had my resounding four-year C+ average to deal with. I admit it, I was lazy. My carefree attitude during my junior and senior years became a stumbling block to my future.

Of course, when you're inclined to be lazy, you're not all that concerned about your future. My entire worldly vision at that time was I would marry my very pretty high school sweetheart, Marjorie; become a dedicated factory worker; and buy a house, and we would both live happily ever after. I was seventeen. Life wasn't complicated. What did I know? Lucky for me, my parents did know.

There was an end run plan available to rectify my situation. I would have to take a special test that, if I passed, could gain me college admission. I went to the mail hall of Wayne University, sat on a hard oak chair with a writing arm, and began to answer page after page of questions for the eight-hour exam. There was no advance prep or study course; I was on my own. I finished within the allotted time and handed in my completed test, positive I had failed.

I had to wait two to three weeks for the results, which would determine my life's course. After what seemed like endless days, notice arrived from Wayne University. I was accepted. My parents were elated; I was in shock.

I enrolled in the fall and immediately proceeded to do what I had done in high school. I paid attention and got good grades in the courses I liked while I half-heartedly attended or paid no attention to the ones of little interest to me. I really had no passion. French was hard; algebra was even worse. Art and English kept me perked up.

My mother thought I should study hotel administration because it sounded like a clean, fairly well-paying job and had some status. Mr. Chamberlin, who lived across the street, was the manager of the Statler Hotel in Downtown Detroit, and she felt he held relatively high social status in the neighborhood and was always well dressed.

My uncle Russ, a semitalented artist, said I should become an art director in an advertising agency. He viewed the ad agency business as exciting, prestigious, and glamorous with very well-paying positions and connections to career advancement. My mother, on the other hand, thought all artists cut off their ears, wore sloppy clothes, and were starved.

My English teacher, Ted Miles, felt I had a talent for seeing things and writing about them. I worked on Saturdays at the Bond men's clothing store on Woodward Avenue, and while traveling by streetcar, I noticed the riders, how they looked, how they dressed, what they discussed, and the sales promotions in the various retail store windows on Grand River Avenue. After submitting a writing assignment about my observations, Mr. Miles wrote on top of the page in red ink, "Have you ever considered creative writing?" Mr. Miles was an exceptional teacher who didn't just teach lessons from books. He took interest and observed his students as only a good teacher will, and with his red-inked note on my paper, he loosened my imagination.

Perhaps the exciting world of journalism would be the career for me. Being sent on assignments to new and interesting places? The status of having my written observations appear in print, read by many? I could see myself as a reporter caught up in the hectic pulse of stories on deadline, typing at big manual typewriters in the newsroom. Journalism might just be more exciting than any movie I'd seen. Mr.

Miles inspired me to become much more aware of myself and my talents—that my future wasn't just confined to the little narrow space my mind currently occupied.

Simultaneously, due to an abrupt change in our world events, there was what one could call an epiphany for me. A new civilian pilot training (CPT) program was announced. Almost overnight, my childhood dreams of becoming an aviator were rekindled. Perhaps I wouldn't become a hero ace aviator like those WWI guys or an Errol Flynn in his smart uniform, but I was now set on becoming the best pilot I could be. I woke up and realized that, rather than just floating through life, I could turn my childhood dreams into reality.

Part Two

Anticipating War

War Might Be Coming

- 4 -

Anticipating the United States' possible involvement in the European war, the government set up a civilian pilot training program under the Department of Commerce and the Civil Aeronautics Authority in Washington. The program was formed to quickly build a national pilot base for the military by administering instruction, which was made readily available through universities.

This was a redemption for me. The announcement of this program filled me with a fusion of spirit and a rekindled dream to become an aviator to the best of my ability, no matter what. After slacking along for such a long time, I was now determined to set a goal, succeed in it, and fulfill my parents' pride in me. I finally had both purpose and passion.

I enrolled in the CPTP in June 1941 at the end of my sophomore year at Wayne. Flight instruction took place at Wayne County Airport (now Detroit International) in Romulus. Ground school instructional classes were held in the evening at the university.

Before any of us went on our first flight, we had preliminary ground instruction. This consisted in familiarization with the airplane, controls, instruments, throttle, brakes, fuel system, safety belts, and location of fire extinguishers and first aid kit, including their use, along with instruction signals. We were warned about propeller danger, running the engine with an empty cockpit, local traffic rules, use of the parachute, line inspection of the aircraft, starting procedure, warming up the engine, and stopping it.

We were learning to fly in a plane that is now called a "taildragger." It had two balloon tires forward and a tail wheel that dragged along the ground. This plane was started by spinning the prop by hand. The prop spinner would get to the front of the plane, spin, and holler, "Contact!" The pilot sitting in the cockpit would turn on the ignition. The technique for the prop spinner was to put two hands on a blade of the prop, pull down hard and away from the prop, and then get the hell away as fast as one could from the propeller. Upon completion of these ground classes came my first real flight in the air.

In The Air

- 5 -

On June 29, 1941, I went for my first half-hour familiarization flight in a tired-looking blue Taylorcraft with a red nose cowling around the engine, a 125-horsepower Lycoming with a cruising speed of 105 mph. Students jokingly called this rather used plane "the Red-Nosed Coffin."

My instructor, J. C. Shugart, was at the controls. Unlike the better-known Piper Cub in which student and instructor sat one behind the other, we sat side by side in the plane. The main control for the Taylorcraft was a wheel, whereas the Cub used a stick called by some in aviation a "joystick."

The course was divided into certain stages, each of which was followed by a check flight. The manual followed the syllabus stage by stage and maneuver by maneuver, making sure you knew not only the why but also the how. Stage A consisted in a minimum of eight hours of dual time with the instructor in half-hour segments, covering the elementary flight maneuvers and passing them before you could fly solo.

After my first flight, during which I briefly had the controls, Shugart entered into my logbook, "Eager to learn, tense, mechanical, poor coordination, skids on turns, slips on turns." It was not exactly an ace pilot review, but I was still determined.

Every morning at seven o'clock from Monday to Friday during that summer, my friend Johnny Carroll would arrive at my house in his Hudson Hornet to pick me up for the long drive to Romulus. I was in awe of Johnny's fiercely dedicated determination to learn to fly. He held a job as a night clerk of the tool crib at Cass Technical High School in Downtown Detroit, dispensing tools and material to the men who were learning a new trade as well as the skilled machinists and toolmakers who were retraining to be members of the anticipated giant industrial war effort. Johnny worked long late hours every night and then picked me up in the wee hours of the morning for our airport drive. When we got there, we agreed he would fly first, fighting to stay awake, after which I flew, and he finally got some sleep in his car.

The primary flight syllabus consisted in training the potentially most skilled pilots in the shortest possible time, a meticulous and demanding cram course. I had finished stage A. Now I faced the more demanding stages up to the final stage D. I was committed to my goal of completing all the steps needed to obtain my pilot's license. Would I be up for it?

Solo And Cross-Country Flight

- 6 -

Being in the air, flying high above the ground, this time with me at the controls was a thrilling experience etched in my brain. Wayne County Airport was huge, far from some little mowed grassy patch. It had two concrete runways for large planes and acres of grass around them.

My instructor, JC, had me shoot a couple of landings. Then JC got out and said, "Take her around and make a landing. Then taxi over to me." He stood off to the side.

My elation was tempered by my fear. All my nerve ends were singing, *Hallelujah!* My brain was nervously twitching. I was trying to give myself a pep talk. *Stay calm, Bob.*

Lining up for takeoff, I applied power and went ripping across the grass with the wheel pulled tightly all the way back to my chest. My anxiety at the wheel allowed no chance for the plane's tail to rise and balance on its wheels. It was supposed to be a three-point takeoff, not exactly a perfect start. Was I petrified? Damn near. The plane flew itself off the ground without my control, and I realized I had to act quickly. I made instant corrections, and the takeoff was smooth, more or less.

Subsequent takeoff and landings went well, and JC, though a hard taskmaster, seemed satisfied. Our course took us through spins, stalls, shallow turns around a point, steep turns around an imagined pylon, coordination exercises, 720-degree power turns while always returning to our base, making a 180-degree precision approach to land and return to the hangar line. And most important and much to my relief was the final OK by the instructor in my logbook.

The last phase of student and instructor training before having a flight test were dual cross-country flights navigating a triangular course by compass headings. On the day I was to make my solo cross-country, I was surprised to learn I was to fly a shiny, new-looking red-and-white Taylorcraft with pinstripes and decorative pants over the wheels, which were aerodynamically sleek molded shapes. My course would take me over two checkpoints ending in Ann Arbor and then return with two different checkpoints, landing back at our base. Ann Arbor was my midlanding point, where an instructor would meet the plane and sign my logbook, and I would then takeoff and head for our base, passing over two other small-town checkpoints on my return route.

It was a happy sunny summer day when I confidently headed out toward my destination. I was in my fancy airplane, passing my numbers one and two checkpoints and reaching my midpoint destination. I circled over the Ann Arbor field, a small, little dirt and grass operation with a nondescript hangar. I checked the wind sock hanging from a pole for wind direction and started my approach.

Suddenly, when I looked below, two guys were running to a car and raced out to the end of the runway I was approaching. They jumped out of the car, wildly waving their arms at me. I thought, *What in the hell are they doing?*

Down I came, making a nice approach, flew over the crazy men, and flared for my landing. Then I floated, floated, and floated down the runway in a perfect three-point landing formation. I kept floating and floating, starting to use up all the runway, and I hadn't touched down yet.

Finally, the plane settled, and I eased her down with hardly any runway to spare. I taxied back to the line where I met the two guys who were waving at me. I had misread the wind sock and landed downwind. The check ride was to make a three-point landing on a designated spot with no bounce or floating allowed on the touchdown. After an angry chewing out by one of the guys, he signed my logbook without making a notation about the goofed landing. Chagrined, I took off for my base airport, landing at Wayne County, covering the assigned flight plan in one hour and fifty minutes.

JC, none the wiser of my antics, spent the next four and a half hours of instruction giving me prep flights, some of them solo, readying me for my final flight test. On the designated day, the flight examiner put me through my paces for an hour and fifteen minutes. Then he signed my logbook. I had passed.

I also passed the ground school exam and the government's written test and finally received my private pilot's certificate.

Civilian pilot training offered a next stage titled "Secondary," a course in aerobatics, which I was eager to pursue. My mother had to be convinced. After what seemed like endless discussions, I was able to make her understand that the more flight time I had, the better and safer pilot I would become. The word *safer* did the trick. Later, in one of her letters, she said, "Remember, Bobby, fly low and slow so that you won't have too far to fall if the engine stops." I smiled at that one.

My parents were both worried for my safety, yet at the same time, they were both immensely proud of me. While they would have preferred other careers for me, like being on the ground in hotel management, they never said or did anything to prevent me from flying. I knew they both prayed for my safety.

Aerobatics

- 7 -

Wayne University didn't offer the CPT aerobatics course. However, there was an opening at Toledo University in Ohio. I was accepted by the Toledo CPT the day before I was to register for my junior year at Wayne.

My parents drove me down to Toledo the following Sunday where I was to report and register. When we arrived, there was no one there. We walked around the small campus, probably looking kind of lost, which we were, wondering where the CPT headquarters were.

As we walked around the campus grounds, a surprising sudden surge of homesickness came over me. I had never been separated from my folks for any real length of time, and I tried hard to staunch the flow of these sudden unexpected emotions. My uncertain state of mind was rescued by the appearance of a fellow my age who, seeing our confusion, approached us and introduced himself as Bob Campbell. Bob was also enrolled in the course and, sensing our bewilderment, said he'd show us the way and immediately took over. He led us to the second floor of the old field house where the student pilots slept barracks-style. I found an empty locker and bed and put my few belongings away.

Bob was an Ohio native and had been a student at Ohio State, the "enemy" of Michiganders. In spite of being enemies, we soon became fast friends to the point that I even learned the Ohio State fight song. That was saying a lot.

My parents prepared to leave, and after a prolonged goodbye, I bravely told them they should not expect me to be home on weekends. My dad said, "Of course not."

The assembly of men in the training group was mixed. Some were destined for the army; others like me were there courtesy of the navy. None of us had any status. We weren't cadets; we were just civilians in khakis. Yet we would lead a military existence, the reality of which jolted my mind the next morning at five o'clock when the wake-up guy bellowed, "Drop your cocks and grab your socks!" That was my first reveille.

CPT training — Wayne County & Toledo OH

The Routine

- 8 -

First thing early each morning, we assembled on the track outside the field house in the cool darkness and ran a mile before breakfast, supervised by a retired army major who was very serious about doing all he could to get us ready for military discipline and the rigors that lay ahead. I despised those early morning jogs around the track.

Ground school started after breakfast. Charles R. Schultz, a member of the Civil Air Patrol, was our instructor. We studied navigation, theory of flight and aircraft, and aircraft engine operation, plus too much more to detail.

Our weekly routine never varied. We were bused to Toledo Municipal Airport for afternoon flight instruction under the auspices of the Metcalf Flying School. I was issued a new flight logbook in which my daily flights and grades were recorded. The plane we flew was a Meyers biplane with two wind-in-the-face cockpits, powered by a 125 hp engine, capable of performing all the aerobatic maneuvers I had tacked to the back of my bedroom door so many years ago.

Robert P. Faulkner was my flight instructor. After my first lesson in stage A, he wrote, "Don't [sic] know pattern and stalls—slow in stalls. Left wing down on landings." His comments on my next flight were no better: "Very rough—poor coordination." From that, I went to "Erratic on landings. Don't [*sic*] react quickly enough." His English and my flying were not rapidly improving.

I was having a difficult time getting adjusted to a lot of issues at the same time. The feel of the Meyers plane was new to me and not easy to handle. Living in barracks-style was a rude transition from the privacy of my bedroom at home, and I was still ridiculously homesick. I never realized I had lived such a sheltered and pampered life.

As always, after a period of adjustment, I began to make new friends; and funny enough, as I became accustomed to the routine, my flying improved, and I soloed after three hours. The comments in my logbook reflected a change for the better: "Good landing—slow in glide-OK on coordination—fair in spins, glides. OK—approval for stage B." I began to get better comments: "Good job," "Much better," "Student seems to be improving nicely." I passed the next flight check and went on to stage C.

Now I was doing all the aerobatics that were on my old childhood blueprint and finding that it was much harder than the ones I practiced standing in my bedroom years ago. Many of the maneuvers, like flying inverted, demanded a new skill level.

When the days of flying was over, we joined for dinner in an old wooden schoolhouse next to the field. The home-cooked meals were prepared and served by a platoon of lovely, motherly women. The fare was quite plain but very good, and my favorite, the homemade pies, were above outstanding.

To my surprise, the two-month training period sped by quickly. We attended ground school and flew daily. At night, we palled around in the university hangout, having Cokes and chocolate sundaes while listening to Glenn Miller's "A String of Pearls" and "In the Mood" along with other hits on the Wurlitzer jukebox.

I completed the last of stage D successfully, getting an 85 percent on my final flight test and was recommended for further training. Of all the aerobatics I learned, the snap roll seemed the most unnatural to me. It required getting the plane up to 120 knots and then rapidly and aggressively pulling the control stick back to abruptly pitch the nose of the plane upward.

Step on the right rudder pedal, causing the left wing to lift and move forward while the right wing stalls. Then you have to pull the stick back to move the nose up superfast to stall the wing. Now hold on. The plane will be spinning at an extremely high rotation rate of about five hundred degrees per second as the left wing flies, causing a huge lift, and the right wing stalls, causing no lift. Guide the stick forward and depress the left rudder pedal to reengage airflow to the right wing. Here's where crucial timing comes in to get the plane upright so as not to become stuck upside down or on its side. The goal is to snap the right wing back into action, getting the airflow to reattach itself to the wing to straighten the plane out.

For some reason, I found this whole maneuver easier said than done. It was violent in my opinion. Perhaps that was just an excuse I made because I simply couldn't get the hang of it. I never truly mastered that maneuver, and my snap roll problem reduced my grade to 85 percent.

I also couldn't shake my homesickness. Despite my bravado declaration of independence to my patents, I ended up going home almost every weekend.

Mary

- 9 -

It's said that if you're lucky, you may one day meet your soul mate. At first, it is physical attraction, and then it's the way you can converse, their eyes looking into yours and discovering you share common ideas and interests, someone you can talk with for hours and never become bored—the person you could spend the rest of your life with.

When I began college my love life underwent a change. Marge Shobe and I had been going steady for quite some time, but at the start of college, we slowly drifted apart. I had met Kay MacKenzie a couple of summers earlier at the Detroit Edison's employee park at Belleville, Michigan, and then met her again while I was working at the Wayne bookstore when she came in to buy school supplies. We casually dated on and off a few times.

In the summer of 1941, my good friends Marian and Reese MacDonald decided they needed to improve both my social and my dull love lives, so they arranged a blind date for me with a friend of theirs, assuring me I would like her. Her name was Mary.

We met for a blind date, and the moment I first saw her smile, well, she had me. She was a beautiful dark-haired young woman with sparkling brown eyes. Her name was Mary Knight, and for the first time, I was head over heels in love.

Mary was talented and smart, and she had the most wonderful, melodious laugh and an even more melodious singing voice. We delighted in our discovery that we both had played in the same piano recital at the Detroit Institute of Music when we were twelve. Even more to our surprise, my uncle Harold had given piano lessons to both of us at different times.

That summer, we spent almost every weekend date at Eastwood, Bob-Lo, or the Vanity—large outdoor dance pavilions on the east side of Detroit. Most of the pavilions were located within bus or streetcar travel, so a car was not necessary. We drank Cokes and listened to Artie Shaw, Tommy Dorsey, Benny Goodman, and Glenn Miller. Many of those great bands would be booked to play at the pavilions for the season. On Monday nights, the Black bands—such as Cab Calloway— would play while many of the local band members would hang out, trying desperately to pick up and copy their uniquely special sound and beat of jazz and swing. That "new" music spoke to my mind and my feet. It didn't matter that most of the places weren't air-conditioned; we both loved to dance, and dance we did until the place would close for the evening.

In the fall, Mary enrolled at Wayne University. She worked at the Bell Telephone Co. during the day and attended classes at night. Her mother was a widow, supporting Mary and her younger brother, which made money tight for the family, so Mary worked her day job to help supplement expenses. I would meet her every evening after class to drive her home and, of course, spend time with her.

While I was in training for my pilot's license, I managed to see her most weekends. I admit, not that I didn't miss my folks, but perhaps she was part of the real reason for my homesickness. Now that I had my pilot's license, I asked her if she would like to go on a flying date with me. One of the things I loved about Mary was her infectious enthusiasm and spirit. She was adventurous, and without hesitation, she said yes. I had saved enough money to rent a plane for a one-hour flight, which was just under twenty dollars, bucks hard earned during those days.

A check flight around the field with an instructor was mandatory for the pilot, after which we were cleared for our great adventure date. My love and I would be alone above the world, enjoying a priceless hour alone in the air together. We took off, and Mary was excited and vocal. I, of course, was the cool and in-control pilot.

After viewing Michigan from the air, I had to show off a bit and brought the plane to a stall and then recovery. It was fun and not dangerous—just rather suave, I thought. The hour passed much too quickly, and all too soon, we were back on the ground. Mary was just bubbling with excitement.

We were together for two years when I left for training in Iowa City. Our romance would have to continue long distance.

Part Three

The United States Goes To War

Pearl Harbor

- 10 -

I was in my bedroom on December 7, 1941, listening to the radio while working on an oil painting assignment for my college art class, when suddenly the program was interrupted by an urgent message from our president Franklin Delano Roosevelt. The Imperial Japanese Navy had bombed Pearl Harbor in a surprise attack at 7:48 a.m., Hawaiian time. Three hundred fifty-three Japanese aircraft flew in two waves, dropping massive amounts of bombs on our US ships and naval base almost instantly and without warning, leaving 2,403 Americans killed and 1,178 wounded.

The very next day, December 8, 1941, President Roosevelt declared war against Japan, stating his famous words. "Yesterday, December 7, 1941—a date which will live in infamy—the United States of America was suddenly and deliberately attacked by naval and air forces of the empire of Japan."

Everyone was stunned; the news was shocking and hard to assimilate. Television hardly existed in most homes, and once we saw the photographs, which were finally released by the censors, the horror was beyond comprehension. The horrific graphics of the sneak attack became a rallying point for the country. Our nation became unified like no other time. The reaction was an immediate, voluntary flood of men, regardless of politics, nationality, background, fame, or fortune. Men from all walks of life, from both the North and the South, lined up at the recruiting facilities the very next morning.

Japan's admiral Yamamoto, who masterminded the attack, cautioned, "I fear we have only awakened a sleeping giant." He was right. The Japanese thought the Americans were "too soft, too lazy," to go to battle—they were wrong, very wrong. The American attitude changed overnight. Isolationists became war hawks, and the American industry began the greatest mobilization of production resources in history.

My CPT buddies and I were no exception. We were eager for action. Reese MacDonald and I decided to enlist in the Royal Canadian Air Force (RCAF), which was already engaged in the European battle against Germany.

One Saturday in January 1942, we went through the Detroit–Windsor tunnel to Canada and found the Canadian enlistment center. We were familiar with the RCAF war effort and their courageous defense of England against Germany. We could visualize ourselves in their smart gray-blue uniforms flying hot English fighters, Spitfires or Hurricanes, from an English field of grass or perhaps flying a huge Lancaster bomber at night over Berlin. We were caught up in the swell of patriotism, defending our country, and no doubt some of the romance—or so we naively thought then—of being in the war, fighting the enemy.

Reese and I passed the arduous written exam that Saturday and were told to return in two weeks for our physical, which we did, and much to our dismay, we both failed the exam. It turned out that Reese had an overbite, and at that time, pilots held a stemlike oxygen tube between their teeth when above ten thousand feet, where the need for oxygen was essential. An overbite was thought to hinder one's ability to hold the stem properly, thus rendering them ineligible for military flight training.

I, on the other hand, needed surgery to correct a sports injury to be declared fit. While playing third base during a fraternity baseball game, I was hit in the testicles by a ball that was thrown by the first baseman while I wasn't looking in his direction. Its impact caused a varicocele (congested varicose veins in the scrotum) and require surgery for me to be considered eligible for enlistment. Nothing like a good military physical.

Guys from all over the United States were streaming through Detroit to Windsor to enlist in the RCAF in such huge numbers that, at the bequest of our government, the Canadians closed their doors to the enlistment of Americans on the very same day Reese and I were declared unfit for Canadian duty. That ended my romance with the RCAF, flying their planes off London fields and wearing their handsome uniforms. It didn't deter my determination to join the war effort as a pilot.

Joining The Navy

- 11 -

After I recovered from my operation, I went to the Book Building on Washington Boulevard in Detroit, took the written and physical exams, and enlisted in the navy's V-5 aviation cadet training program. Candidates who were selected went on to Naval Flight Preparatory School. There was a brief period when I thought about joining the army as many of my friends had, but my preference was the navy probably because I loved the strong traditions they maintained. Unlike the other air services, the navy pilot training program required college credits to qualify, which fortunately I had. Once again, I discovered Mom and Dad knew best.

The navy's active call list was a long one, so I took a job with the *Detroit Free Press*, working in the classified advertising department, while awaiting active-duty orders. Although the spring term at Wayne was in session, I didn't begin any classes because I expected to receive my enrollment call any day. Part of my "advertising job" with the *Detroit Free Press* was to drive one of the newspaper's Ford coupes delivering papers and collecting money for classified ads. It was not exactly the glamorous ad agency career my uncle Russ had envisioned for me, but it paid my bills and allowed me time to spend with Mary that summer.

After what seemed like endless waiting, my orders finally arrived in the mail. I, along with dozens of young men from Michigan and Ohio, boarded a train at Detroit's Union Depot headed for the navy's preflight training program at the University of Iowa. My friend Alex Bacon and two other Detroit guys, Clyde Morgan and Lee Allen, decided on the train that we would room together.

We bonded over the next thirteen weeks while being transformed from civilians to navy cadets through rigorous physical and mental cram courses. "Aye, aye, sir" became an integral part of our daily vocabulary. We learned whom we should salute and when. Officers and cadets "uncovered" (removed their hats and tucked them under their left arm) when they entered a building.

My mom would have loved to finally see me make a bed the navy way—sheets taut, corners folded under, and not a wrinkle on the blankets. She would also have been stunned to see me pass the weekly white glove room inspection every Saturday.

My parents hung a flag in the front window of our home, which suggested that they had someone in the service. It was a special flag, about twelve inches wide by fifteen inches deep, white with a red border and a blue star in the center. If the flag had a gold star in the center, it was a sign that a member of the family had been killed in action.

Iowa Sports Training

- 12 -

Our days were divided in half—a grueling sports program and intense ground school study. The sports programs were directed by the navy's physical education experts in conjunction with athletic directors from various colleges. Bernie Bierman, previous athletic director of the University of Minnesota, was in charge of our training at Iowa. We spent days doing different sports—basketball, boxing, wrestling, sprint, swimming, football—and, of course, marching in close order formation, interspersed with long hikes through the snow until our leg and thigh muscles burned. I was rapidly dropping the flab and increasing my muscle tone.

There was a strong focus on swimming, so much so that if you were unable to pass the navy's tough final swimming and diving test, you were shipped to the Great Lakes navy base and became a seaman second class. I knew how to swim, so that wasn't a threat, but I could see the looks of terror on some guys' faces when they had to dive off the high tower into deep water at the end of the pool. Not everyone made it to the next level.

To pass the test, in addition to high diving, you had to swim the length of the pool underwater in shirt and pants and then surface, remove clothing, and use the shirt and pants as flotation gear. Using the navy technique meant tying off the pant legs, capturing air in them by pulling them above the surface of the water, and holding them between your legs. Then you tied off the openings of your shirt, captured air, and used it as water wings, an instant emergency flotation gear—all done while treading water. We were also required to float for an hour without touching the bottom or sides of the pool.

The instruction was under the command of Lieutenant Bardo. He was a tough chunky, hairy dark-skinned guy with thick, heavy eyebrows that gave him a permanent scowl as intimidating as his cranky deep voice. His uniform of the day, every day, was swimming trunks that accented his hairy dark chest and legs. He wore a permanent look of disgust that constantly beamed at us polliwogs. He would stand at the edge of the pool, sneering with a long pole in his hand. Woe to the poor soul headed for the side to take a breather because the Bardo pole would shove him right off back into the water. The water was always so damned cold that we nicknamed the pool "Lake Bardo." In the navy's scheme of things, the strong swimming program made sense—we were going to be flying long stretches over nothing but ocean, and if we were shot down, diving and swimming ability could save our lives.

There was also an obstacle course in the field house. Hurdles were placed around the track, two eight-foot-tall wooden barriers were erected, and the uphill part, the most daunting aspect, was a run up the staircase of the structure; up the bleacher seats to the top; down, angling for the exit ramp, to the stairs; and out onto the track to make another circuit before hitting the finish line. We had to run the course several times, and while never a runner, somehow, I finished in the top third of the forty or fifty guys.

We also engaged in boxing matches, fighting opponents within our platoon. We did three rounds of three minutes using sixteen-ounce gloves and wore protective head gear and a foul-tasting mouthpiece. Divided into weight groups, we went through an elimination process— the officer in charge was the referee and judge.

In my final bout, having outscored a couple of other guys, I thought I had this match won after the first two rounds. The ref blew his whistle for the final round. We sparred, and I scored with a couple of jabs to the head. Then—bang!—I got hit by a powerful right. My jaw slammed into my neck. I danced back, eyes blurred and watering, and then recovered, and we squared away again. Bam! Another right, this one harder than the first, right on the button. The ref stopped the fight, asking if I was OK. I won the bout only because I took the first two rounds, but off I went, a wounded warrior, to sick bay to be examined for a possible dislocated jaw.

With jaw declared intact, I faced my new opponent the following day. We were two "old" guys—seasoned cadets. Looking across the ring, I could see the look of fear in my opponent's face. Little did he know I was never a very good boxer. As a kid, arguments during sports events frequently ended in a fistfight where my biggest fear was I might be matched up against some kid who had fought in CYO or, worse yet, in Detroit's Golden Gloves, and he would beat the daylights out of me. Probably because my opponent was more nervous than I was, I easily won all three rounds. Pretty good for an "old" guy.

Ground School

- 13 -

We would spend the other half of the day in ground school studying navigation, physics, navy customs, rules and traditions, aircraft recognition (identify enemy aircraft by silhouettes), meteorology, seamanship, and Morse code (yes, the dots and dashes). I had never taken physics, so I had to attend special classes during the evening. Would I wash out because I didn't know what $E=mc2$ meant?

We had to commit to memory the naming system used by the Allied forces for enemy planes, which had very logical reasoning behind it. Japanese names were far too hard and long to remember, so the systems they developed was quite simple. Fighters and float planes were given boy's names. Bombers, recon planes, flying boats, and anything else were given girl's names. We had to keep up with the further refinement of the system, which occurred as the system evolved. Transports would be given names that began with a *T*, and trainers would be named after trees. Last, the gliders were named after various birds.

On Sunday evenings, all of us would stand in a long line in the lobby of the University of Iowa Quadrangle, outside the cadet dormitories, waiting for a turn to phone our family or our girlfriends. While locked in one of the dozen or so phone booths, trying to have a meaningful or even romantic conversation, we were forced to ignore the hoots of other cadets urging us to hurry our phone conversations so as not to hog the valuable allotted time. Those weekend connections were just too priceless to be rushed. By prearrangement, I called Mary every Sunday at the same time, and weekly mail flew back and forth between us.

Because, as the navy knew, we would be exposed to some rather promiscuous situations or more than likely seek them out, we were educated about the dangers of venereal disease. I sat through the film called *Take a Chance, Sailor?* The idea of paying a prostitute was certainly not new to me, but I never took it under consideration. I was still a virgin.

One weekend Mary and my mother took the train to Iowa City for a surprise visit. I obtained permission to leave the dorm and rushed to meet them. I kissed my mom and then Mary, which for me, in front of my mom, was a big deal at the time. I guess you could say I was more than a little shy. My mom admonished me more than once, saying, "Faint heart ne'er won fair lady." The weekend sped by, even though there was really not much to do in Iowa City. It was just so good to see one another.

All battalions before ours completed preflight in twelve weeks and then were given a week's leave before shipping out to the next base. That sounded great, but there was no such luck for us. It turned out our orders were to proceed directly to our next assignment without even a weekend pass.

Before we left, a battalion dance was organized as a kind of pseudograduation celebration. The officer in charge of my platoon, Ensign Gift, asked if I was going. Kind of surprised at the question, I answered, "Negative, sir." Gift insisted on introducing me to a student nurse at the university. She and I went to the affair, and much to my surprise, we had a great time, but Mary was the only girl for me.

My time in Iowa as a cadet flew by fast. After passing all courses, I felt I had made the right choice by enlisting in the US Navy. I had developed a sense of real belonging. Now I had a choice of location for elimination base, called E base because it was just that, the elimination of cadets not capable of completing the program. I was given three choices—NAS Glenview and NAS Minneapolis were snowbound and also backlogged. I chose Livermore, California—sunny versus snowbound—for my first navy flight training where cadets flew the navy's basic trainer, the N2S Stearman. I had never been west of Chicago, and the thought of going to California was very exciting to me, especially after being in Iowa's rather bleak and flat farmland. I was off to sunny California, continuing my quest to improve myself the navy way.

Top. Mayers Trainer
Bottom. NC 21260

California Bound

- 14 -

The train trip from Iowa City to Livermore, California, took an unbelievable seven days—we weren't special cargo; therefore, we were routed on less important trains and lines. When our train stopped in Des Moines, we had a wait long enough to have a whiskey sour (the second hard liquor drink I ever had) and dinner as a small celebration after surviving preflight school intact.

My next "career" drink was in Oklahoma City several days later when our train stopped long enough for us to jump off. I followed the guys, and we each bought a pint of whiskey to take back aboard—bad idea. Once underway, we began drinking whiskey with water in cone-shaped paper cups from a dispenser in the small lounge area. Needless to say, we were soon reduced to wretchedness, our heads hanging out of the open train windows, breathing train smoke and soot, which left us dirty as hell. Lucky for us, there wasn't a supervising officer, only an "older cadet" who carried our transfer orders and was in just as bad, if not worse shape than we were.

Our twisty train journey wound through El Paso and then north to a layover in Salt Lake City where, sweaty and dirty from the train smoke, we could finally take showers and relax at the USO, an organization that provided welcome services and refreshments for the military. They had a piano, which boosted my spirits and led me to play a version of boogie-woogie in my own style, which I developed after my piano teacher (my uncle Harold) told me I would never play at Carnegie Hall. I listened to boogie-woogie records by Albert Ammons, Meade Lux Lewis, and Mary Lou Williams and taught myself, following their rhythmic patterns, developing an improvisational boogie-woogie style of my own. After all, many of the famous band musicians at the time were self-taught. The words *to party* were unknown back in Iowa except for the battalion dance, and I now attacked the piano with pent-up vigor, happy to be playing again, rolling the base with my left hand, improvising with the right, thinking, *California, here I come.*

Exhausted after long days cooped up in the train, we finally arrived at some train stop in the California boondocks where a bus picked us up and took us to Livermore Naval Air Station, about thirty-five miles southeast of San Francisco. The train had rolled through Midwestern winter landscapes and chugged through Southern heat for the last seven days. Nothing could have felt better than leaving the train and getting out of the grubby, smelly sheets of our unmade bunks.

We reached our destination during an early spring rain. I stood mesmerized, transfixed by the rolling verdant California hills that profiled the handsome brilliant yellow Stearmans flying overhead, all in formation for a landing. The field's control tower had turned on the recall light—a powerful rotating red beacon, signaling all planes to return to base. The air was filled with yellow biplanes; the scene was almost dreamlike to me. As I watched them, I told myself I had made it far enough to finally fly one of those planes.

Hotel California

- 15 -

The air station was simple in its layout. One long street began at the entrance to the base, manned by navy and marine guards. It then turned left past administration and the flight building where the daily flight schedule was posted. The control tower was located on the top story. Air traffic was visually directed because there was no radio contact with the Stearmans. The street ran parallel to the flight line and the field, one side of the street housing the barracks and mess hall along with the bachelor officers' quarters at the end. On the other side of the street was the tarmac, where the Stearmans were lined up and tied down.

Primary training was similar to CPT secondary aerobatics. But this was the navy's far more sophisticated version, much more technical and precise. In addition, there would be night flying, a whole new experience for me.

I thought four in a room in my previous quarters was crowded; now I was housed on the second floor of the cadet barracks. There were sixty cadets jabbering, laughing, belching, sleeping on two-man tubular steel bunks—stacked male bodies belching, snoring, farting, and getting dressed and undressed all in one room. The bunks were assigned in alphabetical order. The guy before me was Cadet Hanson; the guy after me was Cadet Hurd.

I was now among California guys, who were a whole lot different from Midwesterners. First, they were all tan, very tan. Second, they were toned and fit, not that I wasn't but they had that natural outdoor, rugged, poster boy look. One of the guys could easily not only reach down and stand on his hands with no effort but continue to walk on them across the room as well, which of course impressed me. I asked him where he learned to do that and got a short, terse, "At the beach, of course." *Stupid question* was more or less implied.

Their lives centered on the ocean, and they seemed to be full of fun and carefree as birds, only concerned about the now and the moment. I wondered if they gave any serious thought to why we were there and what our future would be like in a very short time at war. In retrospect, perhaps they had the right attitude—live life to the fullest, at the moment.

I noticed a series of safety cartoons posted around the base, centered on a fictitious cartoon cadet named Dilbert. Either Dilbert was committing a ground loop by tipping the plane over on one wing while landing or his plane was spinning around or standing on its nose along with other hilarious flying examples. Dilbert was a foul-up, a dummy, a dope. He always flew a Stearman, and he represented all the mistakes we didn't want to make. The cartoons were wonderful, humorous, exaggerated drawings created and drawn by a very talented lieutenant commander, Robert Osborn, who after the war became a good friend of mine.

The E base was much different from Iowa, much less military with minimum ground school classes. My biggest surprise was we had very little physical training other than jumping jacks irregularly and one long cross-country run over the California hills—so much for survival in the jungle or floating in the briny. We were young and fit, and our real purpose at this stage was to hone our flying skills to meet the navy's standards.

My confidence was high and my spirit positive. I was here to ready myself for the next challenge—to fly one of the best training aircraft ever designed, the Stearman.

Time For Fun

- 16 -

Given weekend liberty, I usually headed to San Francisco by bus or hitchhiking. I was captured by the magic of this port city of hills and cable cars. While roaming the streets, climbing up and down the hills, and admiring the Victorian houses, I could understand why so many people romanticize this place. It was a long way and totally different from a city like Detroit, and I felt I could love living in California rather than Michigan.

I struck up a friendship with one of the California cadets and realized perhaps I had stereotyped some of my new alphabetical friends. My new pal, Henry Jones, had pale skin and freckles. He was tall and thin and had a keen interest in cars as did I. I was impressed that he had built his own hot rod—a very California car guy. We went on liberty together, and at one point, he introduced me to friends of his family who had an attractive daughter. Allowed the use of her family's Lincoln—quite a step up from my dad's secondhand Dodge—we went out to dinner several times and found we enjoyed each other's company a lot. But Mary was always on my mind.

Cadet Hudson and I also became hitchhiking pals, and one particular time, a very attractive young woman stopped her car to pick us up. Now Hudson was tall and well built, and I had the enviable opportunity to watch and listen to a smooth California guy go to work. Oh, I forgot to mention that Hudson also had tousled blond hair, sun-kissed California skin, and a picture-perfect smile. It took him no time at all to hit his personality button, and by the time we got to Frisco, he had a date with what's-her-name to go to the Mills College student-alumni dance. She assured me (Mr. Tag-Along) she could get a blind date for me as well.

On the appointed evening, what's-her-name met us at the door, and Hudson promptly danced off with her while I waited in the lobby—no date in sight. An older alumna called "upstairs" to see if anyone wanted to go to the dance. Yes! "Be seated." She fluttered and gushed. "She'll be down in just a few minutes."

A young woman dying to attend the dance had fate intervene in her life—a navy cadet in uniform awaiting her below. In about twenty minutes, she appeared in, I must say, a very fetching gown. Alice (let's call her Alice) was an unattractive woman who would have been fine with me if she could have at least carried on some kind, any kind, of conversation. Alice was editor of the school newspaper, and her entire conversation consisted in "Look, there's so-and-so with so-and-so. Doesn't she look pretty?" Totally uninteresting. I could tell right from the start it was going to be a long, long evening.

To make matters worse, for someone who loved to dance as much as I did, she was a very poor dancer. I fell into this boring long evening trap, thanks to Hudson, who was having the time of his life dancing away the entire evening with what's-her-name. Did I mention that Hudson coaxed me into smoking my first cigarette? What a devil.

The N2s-4 Stearman

- 17 -

The Stearman biplane (also referred to as Kaydet) was one of the most recognized trainers of all time during the 1930s and 1940s. Over eight thousand of these planes were built in the United States specifically for the war effort. Painted a bright yellow, powered by a 220 hp Lycoming R-689 engine, it was dubbed "the Yellow Peril." The majority of pilots training to fly were required to solo in this aircraft before receiving their aviator wings. I was now starting to learn to fly the exacting navy way on this magnificent aircraft.

We were issued flight gear, the first evidence that we were truly naval aviation cadets—a tan cloth helmet, goggles, and a light summer flight jacket. I was issued a new logbook, which stayed with me during this phase. It was my official flight record and, like the previous ones, included type of plane, plane number, date, and whether it was a solo flight or dual with an instructor or passenger, night or day flight. Flight time was recorded in hours and tenths, plus my cumulative flight time.

Every morning we marched in formation to the flight line, where we checked the day's schedule. For the first part of training, stage A, we spent two days covering visual reference, relation of wind direction, visually scanning around for enemy aircraft while flying, throttle coordination, use of stabilizer (trim tab), taxiing and brakes, field rules, and safety.

My first check ride was with Lieutenant Scholl. Our in-air communication was via the Gosport tube—a hoselike apparatus that went from the back seat, where the instructor sat, to the front cockpit, where I was. In two cockpit biplanes, the pilot flying the plane almost always sat in the back. Part of the reason was that the visibility is better, and that seat is nearer the center of gravity from which, in theory, you get a better feel for the plane.

At my end of the Gosport, the tube split in two, the ends of which I plugged into the ear openings on my helmet. Lieutenant Scholl held the other end and spoke into it, telling me what maneuver he wanted me to do, where to go, what I had done wrong, suggestions, and so on. It was a one-way conversation. We took off over the early spring-green northern California hills and leveled off at five thousand feet. After demonstrating some turns and the plane's behavior in a stall, he turned the controls over to me and instructed me to perform certain basic maneuvers.

This plane not only felt powerful but was much more substantial than the Meyers, which I had previously flown. It was very stable and quickly responsive and felt very muscular; plus, I found it fun to fly. I hadn't flown for a few months, yet it felt completely natural to me as though I hadn't missed a beat being in the air. Whatever rust I thought I had acquired was shed very quickly.

We landed, and Scholl gave me an "up." Now I was to begin stage B. The syllabus was precision, a word that underscores every phase of navy flight training. Stage B subjects included high-altitude forward slips, precision circle landings, S turns, advanced turns, wingovers, chandelles, precision circle landings, slips, pylon eights, small field procedure, and the end-stage check flight. For some reason, my instructor, Lieutenant Scholl, doesn't stand out in my mind after all these years, yet I have a vivid memory of my next instructor for stage B training—Ensign Perkins.

Perkins

- 18 -

I used the deferential phrase "yes, sir" as appropriate when I met Ensign Perkins, my new instructor, for the first time. Perkins was probably in his late twenties or early thirties, though due to the length of time it's hard for me to conjure up his image. He had dark hair, a dark complexion, and very manly features. He was quiet, sharply observant, and laid back with a typical slow Texas drawl—the perfect teacher for me. Some instructors hollered while using obscenities as a form of communication and didn't hesitate to use the control stick on occasion to impatiently whack knees. That wasn't Perkins's style.

I was now in the phase of building up both solo practice time and precision—a word I may repeat many times because it underscores every phase of navy flight training. One day after Perkins demonstrated and I practiced small field procedure slips in an outlying grass field, he taxied back to the takeoff position. He said over the Gosport in his slow drawl, "How'd ya like to flah under those telephone wires at the end ah the field?" He looked at me with a sly, mischievous grin on his face. I heard the daredevil in his voice, and I responded with an enthusiastic thumbs-up.

Perkins gunned the Stearman, applying full power; we raced across the little field and lifted off, wheels just above the grass, arrow straight, whizzing toward the phone lines hanging from the poles. Zooming along this close to the ground, the sensation of speed was more exciting than anything I'd experienced before. I watched, trying to estimate the space between the ground and the wires—decisions Perkins was making in split seconds without any hesitation, flying crop-duster-style. My eyes kept flicking up and down between the wires and the grass. In a flash and blur of dark lines, we shot beneath the wires and pulled up into the sky, having cheated fate with foolish but skillful daring. At that moment, we were just two navy guys breaking the rules, burnishing our bravado, and having a hell of a good time.

Final Phase At Livermore

- 19 -

Precision—and I repeat, precision, the basis of the navy's flight training—was drilled into us each day. Advanced turns, slips, wingovers, chandelles, circle slips, loops, slow rolls, Immelmann turns, snap rolls—all of them were practiced over and over. We must have absolute control of the plane regardless of weather, night or day, landing on a field or practice landing on a carrier; we flew nonstop.

At one point during a training session, Perkins set the brakes, got out, and said, "Take the back seat." This gesture came totally unexpected. It was an unspoken ritual in a navy rich with tradition. We exchanged positions and meaningful glances. I understood with pride the significance of the act, small as it was but large in concept. It was an initiation of sorts—the qualified instructor acknowledging his student's skill. It was another step toward becoming a navy fighter pilot, and I was silently bursting with pride and confidence as I got into the back seat, taxied to the end of the field, squared away, applied power, and took off, flying us back to NAS Livermore.

I had now received "ups" on stages B and C and was ready to advance to the final stage D and two new aspects of flight, night flying and formation flying. After an hour of night familiarization flight with Ensign Gillette, I was exposed for the first time to an unfamiliar dark aerial world. We landed, and Gillette then sent me out into the night solo. I took off, gained altitude, and flew to my designated airspace, nervous as hell, keeping an eye out for the location of the field, my reference point, other planes, and the dim, irregular mountain horizon—all the while not really enjoying myself. With few ground lights for comfort, what were familiar instruments in the daylight now became evil-looking objects conspiring to deceive me, conjuring up some long-forgotten childhood fears of the dark from the depths of my subconscious.

Finally, it was back to the field, the air full of other cadets finishing their nighttime. The large rectangular macadam surface allowed several planes to land at the same time, taxi forward, and turn left on the taxiway back to the flight line. I landed cautiously, relieved to be back on terra firma and in Edison's world of light.

The last and final phase was formation flying—three planes in a V formation to experience flying in proximity to other planes while maintaining position. It wasn't that difficult as long as the leader wasn't a throttle jockey. My former CPT training accelerated my progress at Livermore. I completed all the training phases, getting "ups" in each of the four check flights, and finished E base in four and a half weeks.

Now I was headed to NAS Corpus Christi, Texas, the navy's Western equivalent of Pensacola, Florida. I left my good-looking tan California friends and the "alphabetical" platoon behind.

Texas

- 20 -

Basic and instrument training was conducted at Corpus's two outlying fields, Beeville and Cabiniss. The Naval Bureau of Aeronautics had prefix designation for each aircraft type. The SNV's designation was S for trainer, N for navy, and V for Vultee, the manufacturer. This was the plane used for our next stage of trainer time, instrument flying, formation flying, and night flying. The plane was a major step to a more complicated higher-performance aircraft with its 450 hp Pratt & Whitney engine.

We were also assigned time on the Link Trainer, which was a mechanical cockpit (a forerunner of today's flight simulator) connected to a machine that could turn the stubby dark blue device up, down, and side to side by use of controls in the cockpit. It had a full set of basic instruments and a stick. It had a hood that closed over the pilot, who was expected to fly only on instruments without visual reference. An instructor monitored the pilot's performance, setting up radio signal courses to be flown. It was possible to stall the Link and crash but not burn. It was difficult to master the odd feeling of flying mechanically sitting in a chair with both feet on the ground.

The SNV Valiant was nicknamed the "Vultee Vibrator" by most of the airmen because the canopy rattled when the engine was running, and it shuddered in the second and third turns of a tailspin. In spite of its questionable nickname, it was fun to fly a heavier, more sophisticated, more complex aircraft. It cruised at 130 mph and had a two-way radio and a two-position variable pitch propeller, plus landing flaps, but the landing gear was fixed as the wheels did not retract.

In addition to training in the Vibrator, we attended the boring instrument-training sessions. Most days consisted of planes taking off to keep below a specific altitude until passing a certain field point while incoming planes had to keep above a specific altitude, resulting in the crisscrossing of aircrafts. It was wild and somewhat hairy but still kind of boring.

Unlike all other flight training up to this point, I never had the same instructor from day to day, creating a feeling of detachment. I suppose I could compare it to sitting at the Link Trainer, somewhat disembodied.

From time to time, cadets would be asked to fill out forms that always asked for preferred burial location (Arlington Cemetery or hometown), next of kin, and our flying preference in rank order as follows:

OBSERVATION

Flying the OS2U Kingfisher, a scout floatplane which was carried aboard heavy cruisers equipped with a catapult.

AMPHIBIOUS PATROL

Training in the workhorse PBY Catalina.

DIVE-BOMBERS, TORPEDO BOMBERS, OR FIGHTERS

Never losing sight of my goal, I always picked as my number one choice fighters, with the dive-bombers and torpedoes a distant second and third.

Hardy Holloway

- 21 -

By surprise while at Cabiniss Field, I bumped into Cadet Harding "Hardy" Holloway. He was also from Detroit and had attended Northwestern High School; plus, he was a friend of some of my fraternity brothers who had gone to Northwestern. Hardy was fun to be with. He was one of those guys who lived every moment with exuberant passion, which rubbed off on anyone around him.

Hard was short in stature, muscular, loud by nature, athletic, and balding—yes, balding. Though he was a cadet, he was already a marine at heart, and he spoke of it to no end. He loved the marines and was as passionate about it like he was with just about everything in his life.

Cadets were allowed to opt for the Marine Corps before receiving their commission. I considered that option some time ago in a letter to my parents. My father wrote back, "Stay on course—the Naval Air Corps." My dad reaffirmed my decision.

Hard and I proceeded through basic at the same time, often being able to team up and fly formation on each other. We had some good times grinning from plane to plane as we flew to and from outlying fields and shoot touch-and-go landings in the Vibrators.

Holloway's dad seemed to exert a strong influence on him. I noticed he spoke of him quite often in very tender and admiring terms. His father had friends in Corpus, and being proud of Harding's accomplishments, he asked Hardy to pay them a social visit and introduce himself. After establishing phone contact, Hardy was invited by his father's friends to attend church on Sunday, followed by lunch at their home. I could see Hardy was nervous and pretty uncomfortable about this meeting with people he didn't even know when he asked me if I would go with him for moral support. I said, "Of course, I would."

We made a plan. It wasn't terribly creative, but we agreed that if either of us wanted to leave at any time during this social occasion, we would scratch our nose several times with the excuse that it was time to return to base. We met at the Baptist church of his father's friend in a very small and simple white building. It was Texas. It was hot as it can get in Texas.

The small completely filled chapel was stifling. It was my first exposure to a Baptist service. Having been raised Episcopal, the service was completely foreign to me. The music and singing were great and most uplifting, but I wasn't accustomed to what seemed like endlessly long biblical sermons and loud vocal emotional responses.

After the service, we went to lunch held in our host's home, which consisted of quite a spread of fine Southern-style cooking. After all the introductions, the conversation turned to Hardy's father, the war, our military training, and Texas. All the women were dressed in long white dresses. I wasn't sure if that was due to the season, the heat, or the religion, and they were very quiet. As a matter of fact, they hardly spoke at all.

We enjoyed the food, and just when the conversation became more than tedious, I saw Hardy scratch his nose—hard. We told our hosts that, regretfully, it was time to return to the base; and after a profuse thank-you, we left. With Hardy's obligation over, we made our way back to base and headed straight for a movie—any movie.

Like so many friendships during military training, our paths diverged, which was inevitable. So many periods of friendships became marked in our mind's logbook, like another flight checked and passed with esteem.

The SNJ

- 22 -

Our next step of specific, designated training took place at NAS Kingsville, Texas, where the King Ranch seemed as big as the state. Now I would be flying SNJs—a two-seater 600 hp, closed cockpit trainer with hydraulically retractable landing gear and flaps to help slow the landing speed. The syllabus included gunnery, tactics, night flying, cross-country navigation, formation flying, and bombings— using small smoke bombs. The navy's nickname for the SNJ was the "Texan." Flying one was a large step up the ladder.

Our flight group had been on a navigation exercise—each of us taking turns leading the group, flying the designated course plotted on our navigation boards. Upon returning to the field, while on the upwind leg of the traffic pattern at about 300 feet, my engine quit. *Oh shit!* I switched the fuel selector to reserve and worked the wobble pump rapidly to bring up fuel pressure. The prop was dead. It wouldn't catch.

I was starting down, losing speed. I saw an empty runway to my left. Banking toward it, keeping the nose down in a shallow glide while checking my airspeed, I aimed for the end of the concrete of the landing field. No time for panic now.

Large heavy planes are not meant to be gliders, and I would stall if lift was lost. If that happened, the plane would shudder, drop a wing, flip over, crash, and most likely burn. I had split-second images of not only my career as a fighter pilot being over but me being over as well.

I had enough altitude to keep the plane sliding above stalling speed and thought there was enough glide slope to pass over the hangars and parked planes. Things were happening so fast that there didn't seem to be time to think—I reacted on gut instinct. The control tower barked at me, "Take a wave off! Plane coming down on runway 8! Wave off! Apply power and go around." Yeah, great advice, but there was no damn power!

Now realizing the emergency, the tower then hollered to all planes on approach, "Clear the runway! Go around!"

I would have to make a crosswind landing—the wind coming from my right instead of straight ahead. My correction would be crabbing, heading into it a little. Back pressure on the stick, I flared out of the glide, straightened, and set the plane down on a three-point landing at the beginning of the runway, gently applying the brakes to come to a stop well before the intersection of the active runway.

My mind was spinning. I was sure I had just washed myself out of the program, but I hadn't made a mistake. I began to rationalize. I ran out of gas, so it wasn't my fault. Yet deep down, I knew there were no excuses. I had screwed up. "Fly low and slow." Right, Mom?

A truck picked me up, and I was ordered to the officer of the day's office. Standing in front of his desk, the lieutenant on duty asked me for an explanation. I said, "I ran out of gas and switched to reserve as soon as the engine quit, sir."

He sternly asked, "Do you fully understand the fuel system?"

I responded, "Yes, sir."

He then handed me a pen and paper and replied, "Draw me a diagram of it."

I did—it was wrong. There was no separate reserve tank. It was part of the right tank I had emptied—pilot error for not switching to the left tank earlier, which was full. I learned then and there that the word *assume* can make an ass out of you.

The lieutenant then called upon the yeoman who was present and had given us instructions on the fuel system when we first arrived at Kingsville to clearly repeat those instructions to me in front of everyone. Just when I thought it couldn't get any worse, an excited flight instructor burst into the room, headed for the OOD, and burst out, saying, "Man! Did you see that great dead stick landing that just came in a while ago?" The OOD gave him a hard look and shushed him, nodding in my direction.

Had I not made a mistake, I wouldn't have had to land that heavy bird like a feather coming down in a meadow. My head was in conflict. I had made a mistake, yet I had corrected it with skill. It was almost like an algebra problem where two wrongs somehow turn out to become the right answer. It was strange to feel both proud and ashamed.

Wings Of Gold

- 23 -

The base had a couple of "shame signs" made of wood, with holes drilled on each side and a rope to be hung around the neck like huge necklaces on errant cadets. My sign, a Maltese cross, was about twelve inches square and said, "I was a friend of Hitler." I wondered why they didn't hang a Hirohito sign on me as I was sure I would be headed for the Pacific.

I had to wear the damned thing for a week whenever I wasn't flying. As the week passed, I regained composure and took it in good stride with a sense of humor, feeling less ashamed and actually proud of having come out of a gross error as well as I did. At least I hadn't washed out. There were guys who, at this last stage, were declared a poor risk for continued flight training. It didn't happen that often, but when it did, it had to be devastating for the person who had put so much time and hard effort into getting this far.

Days spent in the air were pure satisfaction and became less and less stressful. Evenings found us hanging out in the cadets' lounge, having Cokes, writing letters, and listening to the Mills Brothers and big bands on the Wurlitzer. Mary and I still corresponded weekly, and we were both looking forward to my upcoming leave.

My days as a cadet were dwindling with my graduation nearing. I would finally be awarded my navy wings of gold. I passed all the final flight checks and prepared for graduation by purchasing my officer's uniforms—tans, greens, and blues in Corpus Christi. My mom and dad got an early start boarding a train in Detroit for the long trip heading to Corpus Christi to arrive in time for my naval aviator winging ceremony. This was a much-anticipated event for them after so many months of my training and us hardly seeing one another.

The first part of the event was a small nondenominational service performed by a Catholic priest where all the wings were blessed with a prayer for each aviator's safety in the air. Traditionally, student naval aviators are awarded soft wings immediately after their final training flight. These soft wings are typically gold-leaf impressions on leather patches that was attached by Velcro to the flight suit. The soft winging was awarded by the skipper of the training squadron.

Then cadets and guests took a break for a quick lunch before the main event of the official and formal winging ceremony, which was presented by the training commandant and a two-star rear admiral guest speaker. Each cadet received his gold wings with the audience applauding. It was a heady moment.

I don't recall the speaker's exact words, but he said something to the effect that "everyone in the audience and the country should be proud of these young men for working so long and hard to reach this point." He stated that perhaps less than 10 percent of eligible candidates make it through the intense training and qualifications. I was proud to have survived the often grueling rigors, which now included me in that 10 percent.

I looked out at my mom and dad, and I don't have to say my mom was holding a tissue and was teary eyed, and my dad—well, he was just beaming. I had finally earned my wings of gold. I realized once again at that moment, looking out at my folks, how hard it had been for them to accept my decision to become an aviator and my exposure to danger; and in spite of their fears, how supportive they had been. I also reminded myself how lucky I was to have them as parents and how much I loved them.

In retrospect, as heady a benchmark the ceremony was, it was merely a moment, the passageway to a flying life that would become a once-in-a-lifetime experience full of great friendships, demanding tasks, fearful moments, and heart-wrenching tragedy.

Hard-Earned Wings

Three Big Days

- 24 -

After graduation, my parents persuaded me to return to Detroit with them via train. This turned out not to be the greatest of ideas. There were no sleeping cars available, and we ended up sitting in the most uncomfortable seats ever, all the way from Texas to Michigan.

Finally, I was home—a new navy ensign sporting shiny gold wings on the tunic of my summer tan gabardine uniform with a row of brass buttons embossed with the navy's insignia and black shoulder boards, each with one gold stripe designating my rank. I was now more or less in a suspended state. It was a three-day leave. There was no flying, no schedule, no rude wake-up calls, nothing definite except the one goal I had set for myself. I intended to propose to Mary.

I have several sources for factual information to draw on for my story—my logbooks, navy friends' notes—but I have nothing but my old memory bank to play back the details of proposing to Mary. Perhaps I was just so nervous, or maybe there was some fear—what if she said no? For the life of me, I cannot remember that important moment. All I know is she said yes.

I met her outside the Michigan Bell Telephone Company, where she worked, in Downtown Detroit. I stood on the sidewalk, waiting; and when she came out, we walked arm in arm to J. L. Hudson, the major department store in the city. And together, we selected her engagement ring.

The clerk was smiling as I kissed her and put the ring on her finger. There was a happy round of applause among the clerks. We had known each other for two years, and I had been in love with her every single day of that time.

Mary was radiant. We drove back to my house and showed off the ring to my mom and dad. They were more than thrilled, my mom especially since she had already formed a bond with Mary and was now overjoyed with the prospect of a daughter in the family. I was a young man, I had just accomplished the goal of my childhood aviation dream, and now I was engaged to the woman I wanted to spend the rest of my life with.

My aunt Dolly, uncle Russ, and cousin David came down from Grand Rapids to help celebrate my graduation and our engagement. Uncle Russ took pictures; he photographed me with my parents, with Mary, and with Aunt Dolly and David. The pictures were endless. My months in the Western and Southern sun had produced a smooth tan. I probably looked as nifty as my former California bunk mates.

I was home, surrounded by love, happy, and engaged. It seems that times of great joy accelerate the clock. Those times come and go in what seems to be the blink of an eye. That's how brief my leave felt.

Far too soon, it was on to report to NAS Melbourne, Florida. There, I would begin a new phase—operational training, learning to fly the navy's latest fighter, the Grumman Hellcat. I was excited. It was the assignment I had been hoping for and working toward since Wayne County Flying School, Toledo, and all my cadet preflight and flight training days.

Grumman Hellcat

- 25 -

It's worth taking a pause in my story to relay a small part of the history of the Hellcat because its combat success is unique among American fighters, and it still holds records that haven't been broken to this day. The Grumman Hellcat was a major factor in destroying the Japanese airpower. The F6Fs are credited with 5,200 Japanese aerial kills—nearly as many as all army fighters against Japan, and they produced a record 306 aces. Their official kill/loss ratio of 19 to 1 is also unassailable. Moreover, the Hellcat was rugged, with a survival rate of 34 of the 36 aces who flew it in combat.

What I learned later, and found even more fascinating, are some of the behind-the-scenes stories of the Hellcat. In the sudden chaos after Pearl Harbor, pressure was on to produce a plane that could outdo the deadly Japanese Zero. Sufficient building materials were not readily available. Roy Grumman's resourceful crew in Long Island, New York, found part of the solution right under their nose. New York City's elevated old railway, the Second Avenue el, had just been torn down, and Grumman quickly scooped up most of the scrap steel and transported it to Long Island.

A great part of the Hellcat's success belonged to Grumman's general manager, Jake Swirbul. He magically oversaw 20,000 employees in a 2.5-million-square-foot facility, delivering nearly a million dollars' worth of aircraft and parts per day. He realized that the war effort production could only be won by keeping workers happy on the job, and he made Grumman an industry leader in providing counselors, day care centers, softball games, dances, and intensive training programs for the budding, unskilled new workers. He kept the employees satisfied by running the plant more like a family than a factory, even under tremendous production pressure. Simplicity found its place in a highly competitive production war, and his efforts succeeded brilliantly. There were no strikes or slowdowns at Grumman.

Through the war, Hellcats were repeatedly outnumbered, fighting far greater numbers of Japanese aircraft in the air battles yet won against lopsided odds. The F6F was one part of the equation; the other part was the skill of the aviators due to their intensive training quality, air discipline, and teamwork. Many Hellcat pilots had 750 or more hours total air time when they entered combat, and the results showed. They displayed the navy's pride in discipline and precision.

Firebaugh

- 26 -

The trip from Detroit to Florida was by plane to Jacksonville and then by bus to the small East Coast town of Melbourne, where I caught the navy shuttle bus and reported in. I was assigned a room in the bachelor officers' quarters (BOQ) and told to report to the flight line in the morning where I would meet the other members of my student officer flight group and our instructor.

Alan Hardisty, Joe Lawler, Dick Boeck, Jimmie Jones, George Anderson, and I—all of us ensigns except Lawler, who was a full lieutenant and had seen duty flying OS2U observation planes—were designated Flight 64. We were six fledgling fighters assigned to our operational instructor, Lt. Gordon E. Firebaugh, USN. Firebaugh, a career navy man who came up from the ranks, was a member of VF2— the prewar Flying Chiefs squadron based in San Diego. The Chiefs were awarded lieutenant junior grade commissions at the outbreak of the war.

While covering the invasion of Guadalcanal during the Battle of the Coral Sea, flying his Wildcat off the carrier *Enterprise*, Firebaugh's plane caught fire when hit in a dogfight with a Japanese Zero. He bailed out of his plane, legs burned; and in spite of a leaky life preserver and a broken back suffered from the wrench when his parachute opened, he swam seven miles to a small island and then to Santa Isabel. He was picked up on the beach by natives and was at a village near Mufu Point when Geoffrey Kuper, a member of the Islands Coast Watching Service, was informed of a pilot's recovery by natives from Kuper's group.

After the attack on Pearl Harbor and the Japanese invasion of the Solomon Islands, the Islands Coast Watching Service—developed by the Royal Australian Navy after World War I—became vital to that country's huge exposed northern coast. A network of observers was formed to keep an eye on the Japanese. These coast watchers were noncombatant participants in the war.

Control of the Solomon Islands guaranteed control of the New Hebrides and New Caledonia and entry to the sea approaches to Sydney and Brisbane. Working behind Japanese lines, the Aussies truly lived in the jungle. Firmly resolute and remarkably resourceful, they aided the United States Navy and Marines as spotters and were invaluable in their role of the rescue of downed pilots.

Firebaugh's rescue saga took him on a stealthy, harrowing long sea voyage to safety in a patched-up old boat. He knew the enemy well. He was exacting and thorough, and to our benefit, he taught us all he knew.

He was our leader for seven weeks. I liked him because he was direct. He didn't mince words. He seldom said anything twice. He had a square rugged face and lines coming down on either side of his mouth, his chin punctuated by a deep cleft. I can still hear him say if we dared to complain, "I swam seven miles with a broken back." He rarely smiled. We learned not to complain. Everything we were learning and doing was dead serious.

Bob, ready for the Hellcat

Operational Training Group, Melbourne, FL

Meeting The Hellcat

- 27 -

The Hellcats we were to fly were Pacific combat veteran planes, still sturdy enough to undergo all phases of the operational syllabus. The program consisted in formation flying, where I first learned to fly night formation without lights while flying on another plane's blue exhaust flame, tail chases both night and day, gunnery hops, night flying, tactics, and navigation. There was a great deal of night flying, which I still had trouble being comfortable with. Darkness was one enemy that never went away for me—an ongoing personal battle. I always felt lost over the vast expanse of the ocean—a huge black void without some kind or any kind of visual references. It was too easy to experience a loss of direction when you were surrounded by only blank black space.

Before the F6F, the SNJ was the most powerful and fastest plane most of us had ever flown. This was now a big—new, huge step up for all of us. The Hellcat was a 15,413-pound fighter with a 2,000 hp Pratt & Whitney engine, a maximum speed of 380, mph and a maximum altitude of 37,300 feet. It was a fast, nimble, durable, and strong aircraft. Lieutenant Firebaugh gave us a complete briefing on the plane and its flight characteristics, including a thorough cockpit checkout. A single seater, no instructor riding in the back, made it imperative that you knew what you were doing or hoped you knew. Even though I was an ensign and had my wings, going up by myself in a powerful single-seater fast war plane was my true graduation ceremony from student pilot to naval aviator. I was about to take the major step.

My first takeoff is still in my mind. The wind was onshore from the east, typical of the east coast of Florida in the winter. NAS Melbourne was a beautiful airfield, inland a few miles, with rich green grass defining white coral concrete runways. The first flight for our group was under the category "familiarization." Firebaugh was going to land on an outlying field and observe while we shot touch-and-go landings. Navy training never stopped. We were always under the scrutiny of senior aviators whose job it was to bring us along as quickly and safely as possible, grooming us for combat with navy precision.

At this stage of our training, we were expected to strap into the cockpit of a fleet-type aircraft and fly it, period. That meant fly it in fair weather or foul, night or day, in close formation or line astern in a tail chase; shoot straight and accurately at gunnery sleeves; and show our instructor we had some degree, some semblance, of what Tom Wolfe much later called "the right stuff." It wasn't "Mission: Impossible," but it was a stern, serious task; our lives were now where we wanted them to be—in our own hands.

Climbing up the port side of the fuselage behind the wing, using the foot openings and handholds, I had a surge of emotions similar to those I had as a boy on Christmas morning when I saw my toys for the first time—anticipation suddenly turned to reality. I stood on the wing, about to realize my boyhood dream. I said to myself, "This is a navy fighter, the navy's finest, no dream. You're here and ready." Looking back, I know I didn't stand on that wing, eyes to the sky, thinking of duty, honor, and country. I was on the threshold of realizing a profound commitment to myself that had changed my life from a daydreamer to a doer.

I hoisted myself over the cockpit's edge and eased down onto the parachute seat, all my nerve endings functioning brightly, smartly. I liked this toy. Maybe it wasn't a brand-new toy, but it was a good toy, and it was my toy for today.

Hellcat In The Air

- 28 -

The Hellcat had six .50-caliber Colt-Browning machine guns mounted in the wings with 400 rounds per gun. It could carry a payload of a 1,000 lb. bomb or a 325 lb. depth charge, 250 gallons of fuel in internal tanks, and another 150 gallons available with a belly tank attached. Its top speed was rated at 380 mph with a maximum range of 945 miles. An all-purpose fighter, the Hellcat was the backbone of the fleet—the navy's answer to the Japanese Zero.

Each plane was assigned a plane captain who was an enlisted man. My captain stood on the starboard wing, ready to assist me. His job was to "mother" the plane, keep it in flight-ready condition. He was not a mechanic—that was someone else's job. He was the plane's caretaker. The plane was his pride, his life, his baby. He helped me get settled in the cockpit, perhaps realizing that he was entrusting his "bird" to a novice. *Is he good enough?* he might have wondered. *Would he treat my joy, the object of my life, with respect?* Was he praying for his plane's safe return, mine, or both?

He helped me get settled in the cockpit, pulling the restraining straps over my shoulders. I connected them to the heavy seat belt that now made me part of the plane. After he plugged the plane's radio cord into my helmet's earphone connection, he jumped off the wing and ran around to the port side, now forward, standing by to insert a blank shotgun shell into the starter breech that would, when fired, give the engine its initial rotation. The trick, as well as a sense of pride among us, was to start the engine on one shell only.

The plane captain signaled thumbs-up—he had inserted the shell in the starter breech, and the prop was clear. I had completed the prestart checklist for the big engine: fuel selector, mixture, tabs, cowl flaps open, prop in low pitch, radio set to the control tower's frequency, aileron, stabilizer and rudder controls free. I hit the starter switch, the shell fired, and a puff of gray smoke jetted out of the left side of the engine cowling. The mighty 13-foot-diameter, three-bladed Hamilton Standard prop cranked over with a high-pitched groan, and the engine coughed, caught, and emitted a swirl of exhaust as the eighteen cylinders began pumping. My toy and I were ready to taxi. I held the brakes while the plane captain removed the wheel chocks. As soon as all seven plane engines were firing, Firebaugh taxied out ahead, and each of us followed in turn.

One of the memories etched in every man's mind is the first time he drove an automobile. "Driving" this gutsy Grumman fighter toward the active runway made me remember for a moment the early predawn mornings when my uncle Harold allowed me to sit on his lap and steer his Chevrolet coupe with the rumble seat up, driving on Woodward Avenue, heading to Cass Lake for a day's fishing and swimming. I was twelve.

Perched in the cockpit of the tall fighter made all other planes I had flown forgettable. Carefully applying the brakes to steer, tail wheel unlocked so it could swivel, we went one behind the other. Because the pilot couldn't see over the huge nose of the plane, we taxied in a zigzag, left and right, visually clearing the taxi strip ahead. At the end of the taxiway next to the active runway, I swung around, lining up at about a thirty-degree angle, side by side with the others, to run up the engine and check both magnetos, left and right.

Firebaugh said, "Melbourne tower, Flight 64 requesting takeoff, over."

They responded, "Flight 64, cleared for takeoff."

He pulled out, lined up on the runway with tail wheel now locked, powered down the runway, and lifted off toward the Indian River and the Atlantic Ocean. When it was my turn, I made a quick, last-second check—prop in the low pitch, tail wheel locked and steadily applied power, throttle to the firewall. Down the runway I went, picking up speed. The torque from the engine wanted to make the plane veer left—I applied and held the right rudder to maintain a straight course. This plane was damn fast. I was off the ground and over the Indian River and Atlantic Ocean before I mentally caught up with it. Wheels up! I was flying a real navy fighter.

Firebaugh led us to the outlying field and landed while the six of us circled. Firebaugh now waiting, standing on the wing of his plane, he parked off to the side, microphone in hand. We were at traffic pattern altitude, circling the field, wheels and flaps down, canopy open. We circled again. We had gotten our planes off the ground successfully—now we had to get them back down. Firebaugh waited and then said, "Somebody start." It was terse and to the point. Anderson was in position, and I, behind him, started my landing approach as he began his takeoff. Thus began our first touch-and-go drill, our confidence in this fine aircraft and ourselves increasing with each takeoff and landing.

Occasionally, Firebaugh would make comments about our landings. "Hot, too fast."

"Uneven throttle."

"Nose a little high."

Finally, our exercise complete, we circled while he took off and led us back to base.

Lieutenant Firebaugh was the prototype navy fighter aviator—experienced, battle toughened, an excellent and fearless pilot, a dedicated professional eager to share his knowledge. Most of all, he possessed the talent great teachers have—he gave us confidence in ourselves and shared his aerial experiences, a mighty ingredient in a dangerous enterprise.

Flying the Hellcat

The Letter

- 29 -

The first chance I had to leave the base, I took the navy bus to Melbourne and spoke with a person in a real estate office about renting a place for Mary and me. I was assured there were several lovely available apartments we could look at together. With great excitement, I called and asked her to come down. We could be married, and there were great small apartments we could choose from. She said she wanted to think about it.

We hadn't made any definite marriage plans before I left Detroit, but I hoped for a positive answer. Was I trying to sweep her off her feet? Of course. I was in love. I wanted to be with her forever. I had spent the last nine months battling to become a navy pilot. In three whirlwind days, we became engaged. Marriage was the next step. Now I had to wait. I was eager to be with Mary and begin to share our life together. I anxiously waited for her response.

My assigned roommate, Bennett Andrew, had married right after graduation from Corpus. He lived in town, so I had our room to myself. One night I woke up when I heard my door open. Lying there, I could see a figure slowly coming into the room—a man silhouetted by the hall light. His hand reached for my pants, hung over the back of a chair, with my wallet in the rear pocket. I stirred and sat up. The man whipped off his white cap and asked me what time I wanted to be awakened. I mumbled something, and he said, "Thank you, sir." He made a quick exit. I ran to the door and looked down the hall. My room was on the ground floor, and no one was in sight.

The next day, I told Lieutenant Firebaugh about the incident. He said, "I sleep with a .45 under my pillow. You never know what can happen down here. I would have shot and scared the hell out of him."

Each day after flying was secured, I anxiously checked for mail. On this particular day, there was a thick envelope from Mary. I treasured her letters, and this time, I was waiting for the "yes" answer and plans for our marriage and new life.

I tore open the envelope and began to read as I walked across an empty playing field, heading for my room in the BOQ. Her words on the first page stopped me. "You know how much I have loved you." Something was wrong. I scanned each page rapidly, not knowing what I was looking for. Then I saw the question, "Do you want me to send the ring back to you or to your mother?"

Just a few seconds before, my life had been soaring. Now I felt as though I had taken a serious crash. My body was numb with shock. I clumped along the path of the playing field and headed for my room, the pages of her letter trembling in my hand. I wanted to run from the chaos that was racing in my mind. I felt hollow. I couldn't focus. I wanted to scream "no" at the sky.

When I got to my room, I simply couldn't believe or accept what had happened. I immediately wrote her a passionate letter, imploring her to reconsider, both angry and hurt at her sudden decision, which may not have been sudden. Bewildered, I scolded and pleaded, writing line after line. I kept asking myself, "Why?" I poured out all my emotions on those pages. Our engagement had lasted less than three weeks.

The following weekend, several guys were going to take the train to Miami for a short and, no doubt, boisterous two days. They couldn't understand why I wasn't joining them. I was simply too wounded to explain. With some resolve, my subconscious told me I had come this far in achieving my goals, and I couldn't let myself down by quitting. I expected to share all my dreams and accomplishments with Mary; now I would go forward without her.

Training Memories

- 30 -

My operational training memories are vignettes—animated pictures of isolated events stuck against the walls of my brain like Post-it notes written years ago. We flew every day, sometimes several flights a day, for forty-seven days, Sundays excluded and sometimes a Saturday off. After seven and a half hours of familiarization flights, we began tactical training interspersed with a few hours of instrument training in an SNJ before we began gunnery flights.

All of us had shot at gunnery sleeves as cadets. Now we were going to do gunnery runs in the powerful Hellcat, firing at a wire mesh screen towed by another Hellcat, our bullets tipped with different colors to identify our individual scores, contesting with one another for accuracy. We took turns towing the sleeve over the Atlantic Ocean in an area designated as the day's gunnery range.

Getting the sleeve off the ground involved a specific technique—a different aspect of precision flying. The sleeve would be stretched fore and aft on the runway well ahead and to the port of the starting point. A cable was brought back to the plane where the ground crew hooked it to a fighter. The other members of the flight waited on the taxi strip, standing by to take off. Once the signal was given that the sleeve was hooked up, the pilot held the brakes, ran the engine up to maximum power, and then released the brakes. Down the runway the fighter went, dragging the cable.

After takeoff, the technique was to hold the plane down just off the runway while building up speed. Then the stick was pulled back, the plane going into a steep climb. The sleeve would snap off the runway, and the pilot, watching his airspeed, would ease the nose over a little above stalling. And now the sleeve would be airborne, the strong fighter plane pulling the target into the sky, angling out to the blue Atlantic—a drone for the day.

At a designated altitude, the target plane would fly a predetermined course, and the gunnery runs would begin—high side, overhead, or low side, whichever had been stated in a preflight meeting. When the flight was over, the tow plane pilot released the sleeve over a drop zone on the base, where it was then retrieved and brought in and scores tallied.

One day Alan Hardisty had target sleeve duty. He took off and hauled back on the stick, the plane climbing at a very steep angle. I thought he would never nose over—the plane seemed to hang on its propeller, about to stall, flip, and crash. Finally, he nosed over—the mighty Pratt & Whitney engine had saved his ass. I always felt the tow target pilots and the ground gunnery personnel should have been awarded some kind of bravery medal.

The first night formation flight in the Hellcat is, as the first carrier landing would be later, an unforgettable memory—an emotional memory. The requirement was to keep the plane that took off before you in sight, and as Firebaugh led the group circling to the left, you would join up on that plane. The blue-gray paint scheme of the fighter plane blended in with the gray-blue night sky. We drove our planes close to one another, flying on the illumination of the other plane's blue exhaust flame, which lit up that plane's fuselage. Spatial judgement was difficult—it was tough to keep an appropriate distance between yourself and the fuselage you were flying on. The first aviator flew on Firebaugh, the next on that pilot, and then pilot to pilot using the Pratt & Whitney's engine's hot light. Following our leader while following one another became a lesson in skill, confidence, and trust.

Night flying was like plunging into a dark abyss. It was a foreign, unfamiliar world, the alien night-sky world, a place where fear bred anxiety, anxiety eroded skill, and skill battled vertigo—an insidious condition capable of killing the most experienced pilot, the inner ear deceiving equilibrium in the dark with no horizon reference. Practice and time made the unfamiliar familiar, the dangerous manageable. But vertigo could be very sneaky.

Operational Training Completed

- 31 -

We were scheduled for and flew solo night flights, putting in time, getting accustomed to flying the potent fighter in the darkness. After one night's flight, Hardisty told me he had flown his plane over Lake Okeechobee with the altimeter reading zero.

Many times during the seven-week training period, Firebaugh chose to have me lead training flights when he was towing a sleeve or when we were on our own. I accepted my assignments for what they were—my name on the chalkboard of the flight room, proud to be given the leadership that day. I was competitive and always striving. I didn't indulge the trust Firebaugh placed in me, until one time.

Tail chases were a staple of navy fighter pilot training, flying line astern, maintaining a consistent interval between planes. Just as we had maintained the interval while running around the basketball court at Iowa, we followed Firebaugh through loops, rolls, a slit S—whatever maneuver the lead plane arced in the sky. The exercise was a preamble to aerial dogfights.

One day Firebaugh led us through a tail chase over his house, putting on a proud aerial show for his wife. I was assigned the last position—Tail End Charlie. I knew by that time that he counted on my flying ability. As we sailed through a series of aerobatics, seven

Hellcats in perfect rhythm, I found myself suddenly acting like a happy spectator. I was well behind the plane ahead of me, enjoying the glorious spectacle, excited by the air show I was watching, going through the gyrations like a thrilled kid at the circus.

Afterward, Flight 64 had been invited for dinner at Firebaugh's home; and that evening, all of us were introduced to Mrs. Firebaugh. Our host asked his wife for her evaluation of the tail chase. She paused and said, "The last plane sure didn't maintain the same interval as the others."

He asked us, "Who was last?" Of course, he knew it was me.

"I was, sir," I said, smiling sheepishly. I had languished in the rear like I was eating an ice cream cone while watching the acrobats, and I had let him down.

Our flight did have one traumatic incident. When we returned to base and were in the landing pattern, the procedure was to lower the wheels and flaps and put the prop in low pitch, shoulder harness locked, going through the landing checklist—now put to memory. On this occasion, Anderson's wheels wouldn't come down. Repeated attempts and instructions from the tower were nonproductive. He was told to make a wheels-up landing on the grass parallel to the active runway—a serious challenge presented to a fledgling fighter pilot.

NAS Melbourne was watching. Anderson circled, made a good approach, eased into landing altitude, held the stick back as the plane came over the grass, settled, and plowed a neat brown furrow into the bright green Bermuda grass—the plane greasing along like a toboggan at Lake Placid, finally coming to a terra firma stop. "Well done." A deserved complimentary term came from Firebaugh and all of us.

One of the last times Flight 64 went up together before each of us moved on to his next assignment was a photographic flight. A seaman photographer riding in the back of an SNJ was airborne to take a shot of all seven of us flying in echelon formation, with Firebaugh leading. The one important thing the photographer said before we took off was "Keep your canopy closed." I was assigned the last position again. Firebaugh brought us into perfect relation to the photo plane, and we held formation. It looked good from my spot, except for one small detail. Anderson had forgotten, per instructions, to close his canopy. That move cancelled our photo shoot and also the "well done" praise he got for the wheels-up landing.

Those days at Melbourne were happy, satisfying ones except for the one dark spot that was the letter from Mary. The pain of my loss still lingered. I loved flying the Hellcat, but I still loved her.

After completing operational, I was sent to Norfolk, Virginia, and assigned to Carrier Aircraft Service Unit 21 (CASU-21) to await orders for my next duty. Not even settled, new orders arrived. I was to report to VF-13 at Naval Air Station Atlantic City, New Jersey.

Part Four

Fighting Squadron Thirteen

UNITED STATES PACIFIC FLEET

AIR FORCE

FIGHTING SQUADRON THIRTEEN

FIGHTING SQUADRON THIRTEEN

The emblem of Fighting Squadron Thirteen has a significance as simple and straightforward as its design—a flying Hellcat carrying, as its principal weapon, .50-caliber machine guns. The fiery cat's head was drawn for the squadron by the Walt Disney Studios, and the design was conceived and assembled by Lt. George C. Heinrich, USNR, squadron air combat intelligence officer.

Fighting Thirteen

- 32 -

On November 1, 1943, in Atlantic City, the Fighting Squadron Thirteen was formed under Lt. Cmdr. T. B. Bradbury, USN, with seventeen lieutenants, four lieutenants junior grade, and thirty-two ensigns. It was a hardy crew, ready to fly the Hellcats with freshly painted "13" on each. The squadron had already formed when I and Ensign Bill Bowman—both of us early replacement pilots—were assigned to the squadron and eager to join. We were green ensigns, hoping to be accepted, ready to start flying and measure ourselves against the other aviators. I knew several of the guys by sight—they had been in a training group ahead of me at Melbourne, Florida. Included in the aviator roster were also a number of combat veterans, all of us now answering to the newly appointed skipper, Lt. Cmdr. Wilson M. Coleman, USN. The life of the squadron began with the arrival of Bill Coleman.

Cap Coleman, thirty-two, was a native of Alabama and a graduate of Annapolis. Handsome, broad shouldered, prematurely gray, he had a glint in his eye that could turn cold and hard as steel when mistakes were made. But the glint could quickly turn to a sparkle when the skipper went out with the boys as he often did.

Before taking command of the squadron, the skipper was an operation instructor at Naval Air Station Miami. A flier dedicated to excellence, he measured performance based on the number of hours he had spent in almost every plane the navy flew. Yet he was always open to talk things over with the "older guys," who had been in the fight longer than him.

It was winter 1943, windy, and bitter, damp cold. We wore heavy dark brown leather jackets, flight pants, and flight boots, all lined with sheepskin as were our winter helmets. At high flight altitudes, the Hellcat's heater was not adequate enough to warm the Arctic-like temperatures.

My first VF-13 flight was as wingman to Lt. Ancil "Ted" Hudson. Ted was in charge of the squadron's flight operations. Plane formations were organized in units of four called divisions. The two-plane units within the division were called sections. There were the division leader and a section leader. Ted was the division leader in this flight; Lt. (j.g.) Johnny Johnson was a section leader, and Ensign Bob Slingerland was his wingman.

We would be flying high-side gunnery runs at twenty thousand feet over the Atlantic, shooting at a gunnery sleeve towed by an army B-26 bomber. The sleeve wasn't a sleeve at all but a tight wire mesh panel about six feet wide and forty feet long that simulated an enemy plane. It was very similar to the aerial target we shot at in operational training in Melbourne. Our flight would be doing overhead runs, peeling off one by one into a modified split S—coming down at the target from above. Just as in prior training, each plane's bullets were tipped with different bright-colored paint so our gunnery scores could be tabulated after the hop.

I figured this was more than gunnery practice. It was a test—a tryout. I was scheduled to be evaluated as Ted's wingman. Just because I had orders to join the squadron didn't mean that I was assured a spot on the roster. I would be watched while we were in the air. Was I dangerous? Did I use good judgment? In tight situations, would I be an asset? Squadron members were going to be together for a long time through tough circumstances, with our lives depending on one another. No weak links could be allowed.

Aerial discipline was an essential component. Beneath my right forefinger was a red trigger on the forward edge of the control stick's grip that fired the six .50-caliber machine guns mounted in the wings. The guns only fired when they were charged. (They had two modes— on safe or charged.) The six guns were so powerful that, when fired, they grabbed the plane and shook it with their vicious recoil power. Flying this lethal weapon at high speeds and aiming plane and guns at the enemy, in this case a gunnery sleeve, was a complex and serious game called war.

One of the things Lieutenant Firebaugh had demanded during training was that we fly in very tight formation. I joined up on Ted, locked tight on his wing air-show-style. My left wing trailed his right wing by a few feet, a little outboard of his fuselage. The flight went well. I wasn't worried about my gunnery score. My only goal was to demonstrate that I knew how to fly the Hellcat.

After we landed, Hudson's only comment was "You don't have to fly that close." I thought that was odd having been drilled by Firebaugh on the importance of flying tight. Perhaps I was overeager, trying to impress Ted—show him I was a keeper, an aviator. From then on, I eased off a little. I was assigned to the second division of four planes as Lt. (j.g.) Bob Brooks's wingman.

Fighting Squadron Thirteen 1943

Winding Down

- 33 -

The weeks and months in Atlantic City passed quickly. We flew, yet we did manage to party. Not every day was without some fun. By now, we knew one another pretty well, and every get-together of more than three squadron officers was an occasion. These little informal affairs lasted no longer than the dawn of the following day.

They would get underway at the O (officers') club just before dinner and carry on at such elite establishments as the Chateau Renault or the 500 Club. The 500 Club was the site of one (not mentioning names) ensign's undoing who possibly, because of the confusing decorative motif, mistook the bar for the men's room and, much to his later embarrassment, proceeded accordingly.

We ate seafood in Atlantic City restaurants, which at this time of the year were delighted to welcome a group, even a group such as ours. A local businessman, Mr. Robinson, gave us a record player, which later became a fixture in our ready room, plus his large collection of records to go with it. He also threw a smashing party for us at a local hall—no expenses spared, all paid for by him.

On Christmas Day, the squadron received its first taste of action when the entire East Coast was alerted for a possible enemy attack.

There was no sign of German subs, but the pilots were assigned to spend the day flying patrols in the Atlantic City sector.

Squadron life was agreeing with me. Christmas and the New Year came, and the squadron was divided in two sections for leave over the holidays. I spent our brief leave with my family. A bittersweet, happy, and sad time for me without Mary. I still missed her.

The skipper's division, number 1, flew all key hops. Routinely, our division—number 2, led by Lt. Bruce McGraw—flew with the skipper. Examining the personnel of the first two divisions, five of the ten pilots—including the two backup pilots for each—were from Southern states: Alabama, Virginia, North Carolina, Mississippi, and Texas. Four of us were from north of the Mason-Dixon line—Connecticut, Illinois, Massachusetts, and Michigan—and one from Rhodesia, Africa.

In the first division, John Robbins—a Mississippian—was Cap's wingman. He was smart, loud, and assertive. He carried the nickname "Dil," as in Dilbert, bestowed on him by an Atlanta boy, A. J. Pope.

George Orner from Rhodesia made his way to the United States to enlist in the Navy Air Corps. On his way to the States, the ship George was on was torpedoed. The passengers manned all lifeboats, and George landed in a boat where a pregnant woman gave birth. Nature does not stop for war. George was a bright and talented man, responsible for many of the photographs of our off-duty activities. He carried the nickname "Tank," earned after a night of prodigious drinking in Atlantic City.

Ensign Jim O'Donnell was George's wingman, number four in the lead division, a native North Carolinian. Quiet with a soft drawl, he was steady and noncontroversial and wore a friendly smile.

Ensign Fred Griffen was the fifth man in the division. Gregarious and athletic, Griff was a native of Massachusetts who got his share of flights as the skipper's wingman. He joined the squadron in Hawaii, where he demonstrated one of his talents—acquiring material for the squadron. No questions were ever asked how, when, or why. His other talent was bestowing clever nicknames.

Bruce McGraw was a quiet Texan. Mac was combat experienced, having been a dive-bomber pilot aboard the *Enterprise*, flying the

Douglas SBD Dauntless—he had seen plenty of early Pacific action. Now a battle-tempered lieutenant, Mac provided veteran experience for the skipper's front line. Tall and lean with sandy hair, he looked like the good guy who just got off a white horse after shooting the bad guy in a Western movie.

Ensign Nicholas "Smitty" J. Smith III was Mac's wingman, another tall Virginia Southerner. Smitty combined a generous helping of ego with a strong dash of good-old-boy arrogance.

Then there was Brooks, my section leader. Old Brooksie was a twenty-five-year-old combat veteran of the Battle of the Coral Sea as an ensign, now a lieutenant junior grade. From Windsor, Connecticut, Brooks was noisy, short, emotional, energetic, and given to hyperbolize, especially when recounting his aerial exploits. Close-cut black hair and black eyebrows that grew together matched his fierce personality. His brash manner, however, was a mask covering up a sensitive man with true empathy inside.

Ensign Donald "DJ" Carry, from southern Illinois, was an easygoing, friendly guy who laughed a lot and loved a good time. He was the fifth man in our division.

Just because men flew together as a unit didn't mean they were close friends. In the air, we performed as trained, skilled men working together, filled with respect for one another, depending on and having deep concern for one another. Aboard ship as on land, we tended to gather friendships by age, rank, and common interests.

By diligent practice through all stages of the training syllabus and our leader's attention to detail, the group began to resemble a navy fighter squadron. We were still far from polished. While we were learning about squadron life in the air and on the ground, we were also slowly learning about one another as well.

Virginia Beach

- 34 -

We left Atlantic City, heading for NAS Oceana, a navy air base south of Norfolk, close to Virginia Beach, where all three squadrons— the bombers, the torpedoes, and our group—came together for the first time as Air Group Thirteen under the leadership of C. C. "Sunshine" Howerton. Our squadron flight from Atlantic City to Oceana was made during a wild, violent rainstorm that lashed the entire Atlantic coast. It was a nasty flight all the way down, forcing us to fly with a ceiling of less than one thousand feet while flying the entire way only on instruments and visual reference to one another, with our skipper in the lead. Cap wondered later, "I still don't know how we kept together." Our training did us well.

All three squadrons arrived—the fighters, the bombers, the torpedoes—and Cmdr. C. C. "Sunshine" Howerton, who was installed as *der führer* of the domain. Upon arrival, one of the guys—getting his first view of the drenched Virginia hangar in a sea of dim-colored mud—sobbed, "My god, Guadalcanal!" The brand-new NAS Oceana was Mud City. Everyone was ensconced in steamy metal Quonset huts with curved rooftops grouped around a mess hall and a communal bathhouse, with only a narrow wooden walk separating constantly muddied feet from the rich Virginia quagmire.

Evenings in the huts became the scene of some nightly heated debates about the Civil War, instigated by Southern junior officers. As a Northerner, I was more than surprised. I thought the Civil War had ended ages ago, that it was long dead and over. We were preparing to fight the Japanese, not the North against the South. It was my first close encounter with Southern guys, and I realized that they still strongly maintained their Confederate mindset. I came to realize that certain political ideals long done for many are hard to let go for some. I thought about deeply ingrained religious and political beliefs, which perhaps take generations to change or possibly never will.

As we became accustomed to one another's accents and political differences (a gradual change in tolerance), I realized I had some very good friends among them. Their Southern wit and wildly funny Southern expressions (as only Southerners can deliver them) brought fits of laughter, and some of their viewpoints, while different, were refreshing—as long as we stayed away from the Civil War. I did my best to stay away from that one.

When additional enlisted personnel arrived and needed housing, we junior officers were moved into various inns and hotels in Virginia Beach. Dick Huxford (Montana) and J. Renè Paul Parent (New Hampshire) were my roommates at the Beach Plaza—a tired-looking two-story wooden structure yet elegant by comparison to the huts. It was big plus—it had a piano.

One of the major roles of navy fighters was to escort dive-bombers and torpedo bombers safely to their target. We began flying protective cover for them, practicing maintaining position among the thirty-two to forty-eight plane formations, all in proximity, good weather and bad. Two sections of fighters would fly outboard of and several hundred feet higher than the large bomber formation, weaving back and forth toward one another, each section positioned to guard the other's tails—a phalanx of gunpower against enemy fighter interception. This fighter tactic was conceived by Cmdr. John "Jimmy" Thach in 1942 after the Battle of Midway, when Thach and his outnumbered F4F Wildcat squadron were mauled by the Japanese. Called "the Thach Weave," it became the operating navy fighter tactic when involved with a superior number of enemy planes or when they had superior altitude. We practiced this maneuver relentlessly to perform it successfully.

Our schedule took us through the navy fighter syllabus once again. We worked to achieve the perfect pitch of a fighter squadron, developing a cohesiveness, an understanding of our function and flight responsibilities within not just our squadron but also the entire air group. Under the excellent tutelage of our skipper and commander, Sunshine Howerton, we were becoming "navy." We tightened up as a group, developing a spirit and a growing sense of confidence. The Fighting Thirteen was learning how to be a force in the navy's overall air arsenal.

Next step—master the technique of landing aboard a carrier and how to handle our planes once we were aboard that small (from the sky) floating air landing field. We worked diligently with the carrier's flight deck crew on inactive Oceana runways, simulated as the carrier's deck, which now gave the plane handlers live practice in directing live airplanes with dangerous big live propellers. The plane directors were distinguished by their yellow T-shirts. We followed their hand signals, learning the intricacies of real-time carrier deck operations—how to steer our fighters into narrow slots, side by side, and the coordination it took between pilots and the men who pushed the wings into their folded position. The Hellcat's wings pivoted on giant hinges, folding back like a bird's wings to conserve space when aboard the carriers.

Then we were introduced to field carrier landings (FCL). The landing signal officer (LSO), Lt. Casey Cason, and his backup, Lt. (j.g.) Dan Winters, spent long hours standing at the end of the designated runway, guiding us through the precise flight techniques needed to achieve a successful carrier landing.

Carrier Landings

- 35 -

The idea of landing planes aboard a carrier out in the middle of the ocean fascinates most people. It's a subject that has been brought up to me repeatedly by friends and acquaintances, who ask what it felt like, awed and wondering, drawn to the danger and unable to imagine themselves in the cockpit of a plane looking down at what appeared to be a tiny speck of an airfield floating in an enormous battlefield ocean while preparing to land a powerful bird.

The term *precision flying* appeared over and over in naval aviation because it was the basis of the navy's carrier landing training. We had to become skilled at carrier landings, which could be as lethal as an enemy fighter or an exploding shell. A wrong split-second decision could mean death. There was no magic or mystery to landing a plane aboard. It was a skill learned through hours upon drilled hours of practice, flying the navy way.

Our LSO's responsibility was huge—they were charged with qualifying the air group for carrier operations, each pilot receiving individual critiques. We called the first phase of the navy's carrier landing training syllabus "bounce practice." The plane didn't actually bounce. We called it that because we landed and took off, landed and took off, landed and took off again and again and again, practicing until it seemed as though we were bouncing. We bounced for days and weeks, learning the technique of flying a heavy fighter at near stall speed, which was around seventy-two knots, a practice prelude to landing aboard a carrier for the first time.

It was one thing to fly the Hellcat in normal altitudes, rated cruising speed, high-speed bombing dives, or aerobatic gunnery runs but to fly this heavy fighter at a low altitude—less than a hundred feet above the ground, a little above stalling speed, nose high, canopy open, engine noisy and loud, prop in low pitch, trying to sense the feel of the plane in this altitude—was a skill each pilot had to acquire on his own. Textbooks and ground lectures about carrier landings were one thing while you were safe on the ground. Responding to the LSO's real-life landing signals was a whole other aviator's challenge to master. The instant you got a "cut" signal from our LSO, Casey, you yanked back on the throttle, the nose dropped, and you put back pressure on the stick and flared for a landing to catch a wire—the number three wire preferred. Catching a wire was actually catching a very heavy landing cable.

In FCL practice, full power was applied after landing, and you immediately roared down the runway and took off for another approach. Eight to twelve planes would be flying in the traffic pattern at one time, each pilot executing a series of landings and takeoffs. All landings were three-point—the two wheels under the wing and the tail wheel down. Critiques would be issued later.

Finally, after much practice, it was time for test landings aboard a carrier—with six correct landings, you were qualified. The junior cadre were now deemed ready by Casey to test their landing ability aboard the USS *Charger*, and a flight schedule was posted. Senior pilots in the squadron had qualified earlier and were already experienced. They didn't have to requalify, but they still flew bounce practice as a refresher.

The *Charger* was built as a merchantman for the Royal Navy and then converted to a unique single-class ship at Newport News, Virginia, shortly after Pearl Harbor. She was used exclusively for testing the pilot's ability to land and take off a "moving" airfield at sea. In groups of four on a rotating basis, we flew to NAS Norfolk from Oceana, where we stood by in a second-floor ready room, awaiting the call from the *Charger.*

It was almost completely quiet in the room. Cigarettes and matches came out of flight suit pockets. Decks of cards were stacked on the tables, but no one played. One guy paced. Another stared out of the window. Pope was leading the group. He stayed close to the phone, a frown on his face. I sat in a chair, nervously toying with my helmet, goggles, and gloves, eager to get going. Silent glances from one to another told the whole story. Waiting seemed more intense and as difficult as the task ahead—there was no class or ground training for anxiety.

The phone rang. Pope grabbed it, listened, and said, "Roger."

He hung up and said, "Let's go."

Down the ladder on the double, unintentionally as though we were running to battle stations, we burst out through the door onto the tarmac and ran to our planes. Settling into the cockpit, with the waiting over, became almost a solid relieved feeling. Hellcat cockpits carried the odor of hydraulic fluid, not an unpleasant smell, rather one of assurance, a familiarity that I welcomed.

Each of us took off successfully. Now came the test to land. All carriers headed into the wind to take planes aboard just as planes land and take off on airfields and airports. We arrived over the ship just as she began to change course 180 degrees, heading downwind, having reached the end of the operating area she was assigned.

There was more waiting while we circled the ship at five hundred feet, listening for the ship's radio directive to form a landing pattern. We followed the *Charger*'s slow course, circling, observing the carrier we were about to land on for the first time. I couldn't help but wonder what it would feel like, what the sensation would be when the tailhook on the plane engaged the arresting cable. It was an enormous leap from field carrier landing practice to the real thing. A popular cliché after the war was "Gee, did you land on a carrier? It must have been like looking down at a postage stamp." Well, it sure looked damned tiny from where I sat.

Finally, the ship came about and headed into the wind. We flew by the starboard side in a stacked right echelon formation, broke off into our landing pattern, created our intervals between planes, and began our attempts to qualify—six landings. I reminded myself that there were only six acceptable landings.

When I came into the groove for the first time, I lined up, got a cut, eased off on the stick, flared, and caught a wire. I must not have been squared away and properly lined up fore and aft. As I hit the deck, I was headed slightly to port. When the hook engaged, the tail of the plane whipped a little. Much to my dismay, I had forgotten to lock my shoulder restraining straps; and when the hook caught, my head and shoulders went zooming forward at the plane's speed, just missing the gunsight. I just missed giving my forehead a lifelong ugly scar, if not worse. It was like having a glass of ice water thrown in my face, a big wake-up call. It would be the last time that carelessness would happen.

During these test landings and takeoffs, the procedure was, once the plane landed and the hook was disengaged, plane handlers would push the fighter back to takeoff position. Then the fly one officer, standing off the plane's starboard wingtip, would give the signal to take off again. The drill was ragged because timing on the deck between landings was irregular. Wave offs were to be expected due to a possible foul deck.

Qualifications went well for our group; each of us qualified. After the final landing, we formed up and headed for Oceana. The intense pressure was off for now. That night called for a little celebration.

The Uss Franklin

- 36 -

On January 31, 1944, the squadron went from Oceana to Portsmouth, Virginia, to view our new home-the USS *Franklin* (Big Ben), the ship that will live forever in the annals of naval history. She was commissioned on that date by Artemus Lamb Gates, then assistant secretary of the navy for air in charge of naval aviation. He then turned over Big Ben into the capable hands of Capt. James M. Shoemaker, USN.

Assistant Secretary A. Gates made the keynote remarks to the assembled crew and guests. Then Captain Shoemaker, a naval aviator and now the first commanding officer of the ship, greeted the crew and stated, "If anyone had any trepidations about going to war on a ship numbered thirteen, I want you to know thirteen is my lucky number." As the air group assigned to the carrier, we became plank owners, a traditional old navy honor given to the members of the crew who were present at the ship's commission.

My parents were aboard for the event, and they attended the squadron party that evening. The music was great, and why not? Among the plank owners were the ship's band made up of several enlisted men who were professional musicians at that time, including Saxie Dowell and Deane Kincaide.

After final preparations, the ship headed for sea trials in Chesapeake Bay. Cap Coleman received flight orders from Cmdr. Joe Taylor, head of air operations on the ship. He ordered the skipper to bring a couple of air divisions aboard. I had been assigned to the second division. A flight was scheduled, and we headed for the carrier. As we approached the ship, we broke into our landing pattern. A gradual turn from the downwind leg brought all eight fighters across the base leg and into the groove, the space astern of the flight deck, a coarse Douglas-fir-planked surface spanned by two-inch-thick taut cables—the arresting gear—suspended about eighteen inches above the deck.

I made visual contact with Casey, the LSO. Eyeball to eyeball, in visual sync, he "willed" my plane down as I transferred my mental control of the plane to follow his instructions. Signaling with his paddles, he was, in effect, flying the aircraft through me while standing on the LSO platform off the port side of the deck. A high seas pas de deux of reaction, adjustment, and refinement linked by laserlike concentration, it was an exquisite performance fraught with danger. The muscular plane's aerodynamics were pushed to the limit while imperceptible modifications were made smoothly, unseen to all but the LSO and me. Nose high altitude, hanging on its propeller, flying at seventy-five to seventy-six knots, just above stall speed, the plane was now lined up with the deck, arriving at that final instant when Casey whipped the paddle in his right hand across his chest and throat, giving the cut signal just as my fighter came in over the rounded aft edge of the deck.

Throttle chopped and nose dropped, the plane settled in three-point position and banged on the deck as my tailhook caught the number three wire. My plane and I were grabbed by the powerful arresting gear, plane and pilot surging forward, still going almost seventy knots. The sudden slowing was like being caught in a giant flexible web. Now rolling backward, deckhands disengaged the hook, and the fly three officer gave the retract hand signal, telling me that my plane hook was off the wire. I hit the switch that pulled the hook back into the interior of the fuselage and gave the engine a strong shot of throttle to accelerate out of the landing area, which was on the six-foot-tall now lowered barriers. Those barriers are the court of last resort if a pilot doesn't catch a wire.

I opened the cowl flap vents to cool the hot engine and retract the wing flaps. All the arresting wires were raised back into position, and the landing cables snapped up smartly, ready for the next incoming aviator and then a repeat show.

Plank owner certificate
A traditional old Navy honor

Catapult

- 37 -

We were on board the *Franklin* to have lunch in the wardroom and planned to return to Oceana in the afternoon when the command on the ship pulled a sudden surprise. Instead of taking off down the deck as usual, we were going to be catapulted aloft. Command from above had decided to give the ship's crew practice, and we would be the first planes to use the *Franklin*'s catapult.

I was more than a little nervous, to put it mildly, at the prospect of my plane with me inside being thrown into the air. None of us had encountered this experience on a carrier out at sea, the exception being the skipper, who at one period during his career flew a scout plane from a cruiser that used its catapult to shoot the observation planes into the air. "Boys," he said, standing in front of us in the ready room—he always called us boys—"there's nothing to it. The deck crew will direct you into position, push you back, and lock you down. At the catapult officer's signal, you'll rev up to full power and lock the throttle quadrant so there's no chance the throttle can slide back, and then you'll be shot forward. Make sure your plotting board is locked in place and doesn't come out and smack you in the teeth or chest. Once you're set, grip the quadrant with your left hand behind the throttle, salute the catapult officer with your right hand, and place your right elbow on your gut so when you get the shot, you won't pull back on the stick and do a backflip off the bow—simple."

Oh boy, nerves of steel, don't fail me now.

The catapult system was steam driven. Using a large piston, the built-up pressure, when released, yanked the plane by the bridle attached to the plane's underside between the landing gear, hurling the aircraft down the catapult track into the air like a giant slingshot at ninety knots. Back in the ready room, the order came over the intercom to man our planes. Out we went up the short ladder on the port-side catwalk onto the deck and climbed into our planes.

The preliminary procedure for a catapult shot began with the green-shirted catapult crew guiding aviator and plane into position over the catapult track, pushing the plane backward into launch position, hooking it up to the bridle, and then standing clear. The fly two deck officer whirled his right hand in circles, suggesting to the pilot to run the engine up to full power and begin the pretakeoff checklist. When the pilot gave him a right-hand salute that he was ready for takeoff, the deck officer—leaning forward against the wind across the deck—gave a forward overhand arm motion. The launchman, positioned in the starboard catwalk, punched the button that released the buildup of hydraulic power, and the plane was shot down the track, out over the end of the deck and into the air, now flying and then quickly banking right to remove the turbulent prop wash to clear the air for the next plane.

Sitting in the cockpit, goggles down, prepared for a catapult shot, was the definition of high anxiety. I went through the preparation drill and gave my salute, and—bam!—I was propelled forward. The speed rush, the sudden acceleration, was so fast that it pinned my shoulders and spine against the survival pack attached to the parachute harness. The wind stream was hard pressure against my face. I didn't have time to think. I was a projectile shot off the end of deck, suddenly airborne. The skipper was right—nothing to it.

Over time as the frequency of our catapult shots increased, it actually became my choice. I preferred being shot off rather than taking off down the deck. It was instant flying, a lazy way of becoming airborne.

The catapult reminded me of the Shriners Circus my father and grandfather took me to every February in Detroit. One of the featured acts was the man shot out of a cannon mounted on a huge truck. With great fanfare, two huge spotlights danced at the entrance of the cannon sitting on the truck, slowly motoring on stage from the wings. The circus band was small but loud, the trumpeter moving his horn up and down, dramatically leading the noise.

The truck then stopped. The band stopped. A long rapid drumroll began as the crowd became completely silent. The daredevil, Captain Geronimo, dressed in a skintight white suit covered with spangles, carrying a white leather helmet, made his entrance, running out to the truck, leaping on it, running nimbly up the barrel of the cannon as it was elevated higher and higher, spotlights shimmering on his suit. When he reached the muzzle of the cannon, he would pull on his helmet and strap the chin flap closed; and with a dramatic final wave to the audience, the daredevil would slide into the huge barrel, down the length of it feet first, about to become a human projectile.

There was complete silence—suspense. Then with a big bang, Captain Geronimo was hurled forward through the smoke, propelled out of the mouth of the cannon, arms and legs flailing, arcing toward a net, which always caught him. There were cheers from the crowd. Bouncing like a ball in the net, Captain Geronimo waved triumphantly, flipped out of the net, and then ran toward the center ring, waving to the crowd, all the while basking in our screaming adoration.

Our cannon was much more powerful. The crowd was silent, and there was no net, but the rush was the same. I became like Captain Geronimo, fearless because, during our months aboard, the catapult worked every time without fail.

Yet as all things in life, there's never a sure thing. It was called a "cold shot." On one occasion, the catapult failed to generate full hydraulic power; and rather than being shot into the air, Lt. Warren Wolf—in his plane and ready for launch—was not given enough speed. The plane and aviator, rather than air bound, were shot straight off the deck, plunging directly into the sea and were immediately overrun by the full-speed carrier.

This was another rude wake-up call for me. Flying was not just about my boyhood romance with the heroic aces of WWI, who were glamorous and daring, almost like movie stars. We were not like Captain Geronimo in his spangled white suit either. We were simply young men getting ready to go to war, and we were also at the mercy of human error. War is a chain of unfortunate, unexpected tragedies and, in some cases, death, which could happen at complete random.

Trinidad

- 38 -

The USS *Franklin* stood out of Norfolk, escorted by the destroyers *Wainwright* and *Rhind*, bound for the warm waters of the Caribbean Sea to Port of Spain, Trinidad, in the British West Indies. We had practiced as a squadron and then as an air group. Now it was time for the big waltz—the first time Big Ben and the air group would operate as a unit.

A relatively small nucleus of men had been aboard carriers and other ships and knew the ropes while the rest of us were green. We had one endearing and comical phrase—group grope, a derogatory description of a training mission where no one knew where, what, how, or when. Humor managed to prevail among the pilots.

The goal was to synchronize all crew and aircraft for takeoff in the air and landing. This was a massive and detailed operation. The carrier had two principal decks, the hangar deck and the flight deck. Backup planes, spare wings, engines, radios, and other inventory, plus a repair section for all three squadrons, were on the hangar deck. The carrier's three elevators raised and lowered planes up and down from the flight deck to the hangar deck. One could think of the flight deck as a stage that the planes moved on to ready for "curtains up." The takeoff sequence never varied: fighters first, the heavy, slower bombers next, then the dive-bombers, and last, the torpedo bombers.

It was a sunny, tropical blue-sky Caribbean morning—perfect weather for flying. We were to make mock attacks on the USS *Franklin*, providing radar and dummy gunnery practice for the crew and real-time action for the flight deck guys. I was sitting in my cockpit, looking out of a very large garagelike door opening on the starboard side of the hangar deck, admiring the view. The first fighters took off, their engine's sounding as familiar as an old favorite song. Then the barrel-shaped dive-bombers took off, followed by the thick-bodied torpedo bombers.

The noise of the planes thundering down the wooden deck just above boomed throughout the hangar deck as though it were a giant steel drum. I kept track of my flight status by the sound of the engines going down the deck. Soon I would be elevated to the "stage," start my engine, and be catapulted off, joining the command performance.

Suddenly, there was a loud blast of the ship's horn—not a good signal. I looked out of my giant window as the ship passed a torpedo bomber floating in the water, nose down, one wing up, the pilot and two crewmen scrambling out before it sank. After a short interval, another TBF trying to uphold the valor of VT-13 attempted to fly like an eagle, only to land like a cormorant in the warm blue-green water. The roar of another TBF filled the hangar deck as it became airborne, and the ship's horn sounded again—a third splash.

The rescue launch was now darting around like a busy water bug, retrieving the swimming pilots who were bobbing around in their Mae Wests. The language from the command above is not printable. Fortunately, all pilots were trained and timed in dummy exit drills, which consisted in detaching oneself from all the hookups in the cockpit and jumping off the wing into make-believe water. We took about ten seconds to exit a Hellcat, well below the plane's float time of forty-five seconds. We also underwent a cockpit blindfold test; with eyes covered, we were expected to be able to locate cockpit switches and controls, wheel retracting handle, flaps, tailhook switch, throttle, mixture control, gun charge handles, prop pitch control, trim tabs, canopy crank, and lock.

After this miserable flight display, frustrated wiseheads in command immediately prevailed in the brain center of the ship. "Cancel all flights. Stand by to recover aircraft."

The official account blamed the propellers of the bomber fleet's planes. The unofficial and real reason for the fiasco was that the props had not been pulled through since landing aboard days before, causing the spark plugs to become foul, severely restricting horsepower output. The engines were unable to develop enough horsepower to maintain flying speed, so they mushed into the water right after they took off. Rotating the propellers was standard maintenance procedure or was supposed to be. But that was why, thank goodness, we were on a shakedown cruise.

Shakedown Completed

- 39 -

From that inauspicious aerial performance on, the overall abilities of *CV-13* and *CAG-13* improved, though at a moderate pace. Despite all the hours and hours of day and night land-based training leading up to ship-based flight operations, the air group still needed a lot of work to come up to the high standards of performance required for an efficient flight carrier operation.

Communication between ships and planes was essential as was response time when the carrier and the rest of the escort ships had to change course and come into the wind to begin takeoff operations or landings. A deck crash could delay planes short of fuel, waiting to land—asbestos-suited firefighters, usually two, were always on station during flight operations. The choreography of aircraft movement on deck affected the efficiency of getting planes off quickly, especially if an attack on the fleet was imminent. Coordination between all the players in every day's deck drama had to be precise.

Out of the forgiving womb of flying from stationary navy air bases along with the relative luxury of bachelor officer's quarters and the elitism of the officer's club, we junior officers were now novices on the flattop. The ship was our club, and the only defined elitism was rank. We slept in a forward bunk-room, just under the flight deck on the forecastle deck. It was called the JO (junior officer's) bunk room, a claustrophobic narrow width of the ship with a line of forty-two bunks, three bunks high. I ended up in a middle bunk; need I say more? Forty-two tiny safes in the room were attached to the bulkhead for each of us to stow whatever articles we considered valuable and private. Each pilot designated two other pilots as his representatives to open his safe and determine what to do with the contents in the event of his death.

Here was what I'd call another wake-up moment for me. I chose two pals and had a sudden flash of seeing my mom and dad if indeed one of my designated pilots had to deliver the contents. For a second, my eyes welled up, thinking of how heartbroken they would be. It was a brief thought I couldn't afford to dwell on.

Our junior living status was obvious when we would visit the JGs and full lieutenants who lived in eight-man, four-man, or two-man staterooms. The skipper had his own private quarters, of course. We learned that rank, indeed, had its privileges.

Whether in the bunk room or in staterooms, we were all exposed to the endless racket of planes taking off or being catapulted. Luxury existed in the form of comfortable seats in the air-conditioned ready room, lined two by two and six abreast with an aisle separating them. This was where preflight mission planning and briefing and postflight debriefing took place. Seating was determined by flying assignment. The skipper's division sat two by two, and then Mac's division was next, two by two down the left of the aisle. I sat next to Brooks by the bulkhead. The chairs had a compartment for personal gear and a drawer in which to stow our navigation plotting boards, which had a rotating circular center section. We hung our flight suits and life jackets from the overhead hooks.

The bulkheads were gray steel decorated with charts, signal flags, notices, bulletin boards, and a chalkboard where the daily chaos of endlessly changing operational priorities and flight schedules were posted. The overhead was gray steel, hung with the metal battle helmets we were to wear should we be on board and come under attack. All exterior hatches had an extra chamber—to go outside at night, the first hatch was opened and then battered down. Now you were in a small dark space, and it was safe to open the outer hatch. The ship was lighttight.

The ready room was the core of our squadron. It was there we received preflight briefings. It was there we returned after flying. It was there we celebrated and mourned.

Flight operations at sea continued every day until we reached the Gulf of Paria, a landlocked arm of the South Atlantic between the island of Trinidad and the east coast of Venezuela, where the *Franklin* anchored. Each day, the carrier would depart her anchorage, exit the submarine nets, and head for air operations at sea and ship's gunnery practice. The island itself wasn't much, but we did manage to find the Macqueripe Club, which stood on a bluff overlooking a palm-surrounded cove where the moon would cover the Caribbean with silver as far as one could see. Many of the guys would actually pry themselves away from the bar to take in the spectacular beauty.

Training continued for nearly a month while we qualified for the night carrier landings, shot at aerial gunnery sleeves towed by army B-26s, and bombed wood target sleds towed by the destroyers. The dive-bombers and torpedo bombers made enemy attacks on the carrier, and the fighters acted as combat air patrol, protecting the ship. We used a fighter strip, Xeres Field, carved out of the jungle as our land base, flying there from the carrier every day.

The saddest accident, which served to confirm the irrevocable doctrine of landing aboard with all guns charged to safe, occurred when Becky Beckman landed aboard after a full day's gunnery practice at Xeres. He had charged his guns to safe, but in clearing them on the deck, one of the ordnancemen or plane handlers pulled the trigger before the cartridges had been removed. Three .50-caliber slugs tore through the legs of an ordnanceman and on through the flight deck. He never recovered consciousness. It was another reminder for me of how random and sudden tragedy can be.

Shakedown training continued all the way back to Norfolk. After the planes were flown ashore and the squadron released from the ship, we were split into port and starboard wings, each given a short leave alternatingly. It was time to go home, a welcome relief no matter how short a time it would be.

Mom Knew Best

- 40 -

It felt great to be home on leave. My mom and dad were more than happy and made every effort to ensure a good time, even though it would be a very short visit.

I was still stubbornly determined to see if there was any chance at all of Mary and me rekindling our romance. She still remained the missing piece in my life. I found out she was now attending the University of Michigan. I don't remember how I found her phone number, but I did. I wanted to see her, convince her that we could start over. I was still unable or unwilling to accept the abrupt end of our engagement.

My mom, as much as she wished Mary would be her future daughter-in-law, gave me Mom advice. She said I should accept what Mary had decided, that women and their reasons can sometimes be most confusing to men, that perhaps Mary was just not ready for a full commitment, especially as I would soon be going off to war. What did Mom know? I was still in love.

I phoned and persuaded Mary to see me, and we made an afternoon date when she had no classes. Dressed in my blue uniform, embroidered gold wings on the upper left of my jacket, gold buttons shining, wearing my white cap cover, I started for Ann Arbor in my dad's 1937 Dodge with high hopes that this trip would lead to a positive outcome. Mary was living off campus in a residential women's rooming house. I had long admired her determination to get an education, recalling the time she worked at Michigan Bell Telephone during the day while attending Wayne University at night.

I found the address—a sturdy, interesting, and secure-looking house. I rang the doorbell and waited. An attractive young woman answered, and I asked for Mary. I hadn't seen her for over nine months. She came out, her dazzling smile beguiling me as always.

It was midafternoon, so I suggested a drive. We walked to the car. I opened the door for her and then got in on the driver's side, and we started out aimlessly.

It was exciting to see her again, and I was nervous. I hadn't planned any postengagement rebuttal. We tried to make conversation, but it was stilted. I asked her to reconsider, but she shook her head. There was no "maybe we can work this out" talk. She just smiled, sending nervous glances toward me. I wondered why she had agreed to see me. Was she testing her resolve? She made short references to her mom, who had been a widow for many years. She stated that she was fearful and didn't want to be a widow and go through the financial hardships and loneliness she saw her mother endured.

Our drive wasn't going anywhere and became more and more of an uncomfortably silence. I began feeling the same lumpy, confused emotions I had felt when I received her letter breaking our engagement—the same awful despair. Yet somehow I knew during those silent moments that I should stop trying to change her mind.

It dawned on me—slowly, I admit, as most men are when it comes to women—that I was being selfish, blinded by my love for her. Mary was setting her own course, one which she knew would protect her future. I had set my course, and now I was going to war. It was my youthful confidence that convinced me that I would return safely and in one piece. But what if I didn't? I looked over at Mary, who was silent, and I could see her torn emotions. I had to let her go.

I turned the car around and took her back to the rooming house. No further words were spoken. She got out of the car, tears in her eyes, and said a quick "I'll always love you." I watched her walk to the rooming house door. She never looked back.

Mary lingered secretly in my heart for more years than I care to admit. Older and wiser today, as irritating as it is, I realize Mom did know best all along.

Panama Canal

- 41 -

On May 5, the USS *Franklin*—with repairs completed and supplies fully loaded—left Norfolk escorted by three new destroyers—*Twiggs*, *Leary*, and *Wainwright*—and turned into the wind to once again welcome Air Group Thirteen aboard. We were in Adm. William "Bull" Halsey's task group 12.1 with Captain Shoemaker in command of the carrier, heading for San Diego, California, via the Panama Canal—a narrow canal for a very wide carrier.

Colón and Panama City were the main cities along the interoceanic waterway. I went ashore at Colon and bought silk stockings for my mother and Aunt Dolly. They had perfumes and cosmetics, a rare commodity during wartime. Dinner at the Washington Hotel was followed by a visit to the nightclub La Conga, of which perhaps after viewing their floor show it's fortunate I have little to no memory.

I remained aboard during the fifty-one-mile slow passage through the locks. The ship's flight deck extended over the concrete edges of the canal, the huge ship dominating the Panamanian landscape. When the ship reached Panama City, a gang of us went ashore, where we stuffed into a wonderful old roadster driven by a Spanish-speaking driver. When he asked for directions, we made it clear that we wanted to have some fun—meaning girls. The taxi driver nodded and, with a broad smile, proceeded to take us to the Casa de Amour. We had been to other clubs, but none were half as colorful, exotic, or bawdy as Panama's "house of love."

The patrons were met at the door by a bevy of lively, very attractive women. There was a large yet inexpensive bar, and that, plus some music, was the extent of the entertainment—or should I say the establishment's entertainment. The girls were gay, affectionate, and willing—for six dollars. Some of my pals were adventurous. I was not. One cryptic note in my log read, "Met a charming Spanish girl whose name I have forgotten. Quite beautiful and an excellent dancer."

On May 12, we departed Panama City and all its friendly people. The planes returned aboard, and our address was officially changed from Fleet Post Office (FPO) New York, New York, to FPO San Francisco.

Clearing the canal, headed north, our fighters launched a mock attack, taking the army air force completely by surprise. I was not scheduled for the flight; however, it resulted in much gloating on our part in navy's performance versus the army, always an ongoing contest. We powered through the Pacific Ocean for the first time, leaving the isthmus of Panama behind, heading for San Diego Naval Air Station.

When we left Norfolk, our planes were F6F-3s. Now at NAS North Island, San Diego, we were treated to brand-new F6F-5s, the ultimate navy fighter of its day. It had more armor plate than the F6F-3s and was 15 knots faster with a maximum speed of 409 mph (355 knots) at 21,000 feet.

We were also treated to the navy's social stronghold—the Hotel del Coronado, a stately white Victorian building with a turreted red roof. Built in 1888 on the island of Coronado, just outside San Diego, the grand hotel had been host to royalty, presidents, and movie stars. With a large sweeping porch and the Pacific Ocean in view, the hotel was the site of Sunday afternoon tea dances where navy officers outnumbered women by an estimated thirty to one or maybe fifty to one. What chance did we lowly ensigns have? War is hell. I did see Claudette Colbert there once from a distance.

New F6F-5s

- 42 -

The aeronautical advantages of the new F6F-5s included spring-loaded ailerons, which assisted lateral control of the plane, lowering aileron stick forces by about 50 percent. This noticeably lighter touch on the stick gave the plane greatly improved roll performance. Water injection, used when running at full throttle in combat, cooled the engine and added horsepower. Electric starter motors were new—no more shotgun cartridges and, for the first time, a brand-new color, dark blue, with a smooth-finish paint job reputed to lessen drag and increase speed. Mind you, we were excited with our new toys, but they all had to be reboresighted on the double. Newer than new, the planes would be fitted with forward-launching rocket rails, ready to accept six high-velocity aerial rockets (HVARs), air-to-ground missiles. VF-13 would be the first fighter squadron in the Pacific with these fast dark blue planes armed with rockets.

Barely settled, the *Franklin* and its air group was requested to display maneuvers at sea for the benefit of ComFair West Coast. While twenty-four of our pilots remained aboard ship for this affair, the rest of us flew down to Salton Sea for rocket-firing practice. I went to the desert with the first group and almost went on my way to kingdom come. We flew to that desert hot spot—Naval Auxiliary Air Station Salton Sea in the Sonoran Desert, a section of the extreme portion of southeastern California, not far from the Mexican border.

Salton Sea, alongside the Imperial Valley, is 228 feet below sea level, where in June the high temperature was 102 degrees and the low 68 degrees. We were there for two days, after which the second group arrived to join us. We shot our rockets at ground targets—marks outlined on the desert floor, our scores logged by ground personnel. There were twenty of us in the first group, and we formed a pool for the first guy with the best score. Willie Gove won the twenty bucks. I had the second highest score—no bucks.

The routine was simple. We flew to the target individually, identified ourselves by radio to target ground personnel, and made three runs shooting two rockets in tandem on each run. Then it was back to the base, where the planes were rearmed, and then back to the target, back to the field, land, and repeat—each flight a half an hour at most. We completed four flights a day, firing twenty-four rockets.

We were the only planes operating from this small desert base, so we started flat-hatting for fun on the way back from the rocket range, flying as low as we dared on each return. This became an unofficial contest, with each of us trying to outperform the other. The desert was flat, a perfect invitation to low flying. Low-level flying was part of our training but in formation and with a purpose. This was solo "hot dog" stuff. We were dangerous.

We reveled in the excitement of getting down on the deck, hugging the ground unrestricted, skimming the desert growth, the thrill of speed close to the ground. Not satisfied with just flying low level, buzzing the field became standard procedure on each return, giving the air station a private show. We were hot rocks, or so we thought.

One of the guys performed a barrel roll after zooming across the field—a long upward roll along the plane's longitudinal axis, climbing and showing off. Not to be outdone, I decided that I would show up the barrel roll pilot by doing a slow roll. The slow roll was one of my favorite aerobatic maneuvers. With the nose of the plane elevated a little above the horizon, back pressure on the stick, the plane is rolled to the left using coordinated left stick pressure and left rudder until it's upside down, keeping forward pressure on the stick while inverted to keep the nose up. In one continuous motion, the roll continues to rotate to the left, the pilot using full aileron and appropriate rudder control to maintain direction, emerging smoothly upright without loss of altitude, rolling 360 degrees around the plane's axis. I had done this maneuver many, many times before. I did it in the Meyers, the Stearman, the Vibrator, the SNJ, and the Hellcat. I had never done it at an altitude of 200 feet.

I was intoxicated with speed and the thrill that comes with pure adrenaline rush. I went down one runway just off the concrete; pulled up into a wingover, nose up, close to stalling speed; dropped the nose and the wing; and zoomed down another runway even closer to the deck. I flew past the control tower, looking up at the earthlings. I was hot.

Then came my glorious moment—the slow roll. As I roared past the field, 200 feet above the salt water, I rolled smoothly to the left and became inverted. Then the unexpected happened. I had a frightening sudden, instant panic attack out of nowhere. My nerve endings short-circuited. All my high adrenaline backfired. I lost it.

I yanked the stick back and kicked the right rudder hard, not knowing what I was doing or why. I was frozen with panic. When inverted like this, pulling the stick back pulls the nose of the plane down—down, meaning straight down toward the ground. That was where the nose was going along with the rest of the plane. I couldn't think. My face felt completely frozen and contorted with fear. I was hanging on for dear life—a passenger in the cockpit, the plane unleashed from my control, diving on its own, intent on making a big splash in the shallow desert lake.

Sometimes miracles do happen. Suddenly, through no skill on my part, the plane scooped out of the roll. I don't know how close to the water I came, but I was told that when I disappeared behind the sand dunes, the air base crash trucks began to move quickly in my direction. It was a very close call, with only luck allowing me to avoid the grim reaper. I have always regretted that foolish moment. There was no time to think or pray, but I believed it was just not my time.

Dick Huxford's show-off turn at flat-hatting zinged some high-tension wires and put all the lights out in the valley, not to mention the cooling unit that held all our beer. He survived the encounter but spent three weeks under hack, confined to his quarters. I got away with my life.

Breaks From Tension

- 43 -

In spite of the strenuous preparation activity during our stay in southern California, there was opportunity for those who wished to visit Los Angeles and Hollywood during breaks. Some of the boys preferred to spend their leisure at the delightful Coronado or even old Mexico. Others were fortunate and were met by their families, who lived on the West Coast. Some made new friends from old ones at the various parties at the O club on North Island.

I don't know how we found the time, but Joe "Jolly" Maguire, I, and some of the others scouted around pawn or used shops until we found a number of musical instruments—saxophones, trumpets, guitars, and a clarinet, some of which were contributed by one of the swell women's volunteer organizations. We couldn't find a drum, which was imperative, so I laid out forty bucks at a secondhand store, which completed our quest. In our squadron, we had Maguire, a former one-night stand dance man; Heinrich, who among other proclivities had run a nightclub; and Stilwill, who had spent considerable time on the radio. With the help and enthusiasm of the rest of the squadron, we cooked up a series of ready room entertainment gigs, which were a joy to behold, at least we thought so. Those horns and drums took on an importance for all of us that is hard to describe.

The squadron guys formed a seven-piece band. I was on the drums, Jolly Maguire and Sully on the saxes, Carpenter on the trumpet, McKinney and Miller on the guitars, and Martin on the clarinet. Others sat in from time to time. The vocals were supplied by the skipper, who rendered "The Sheik" loud, lustily, and often; Martin, whose "Daddy" was always a favorite; and Stilwill, who added a spiritualistic quality to "Red Wing," plus Weidman, whose "Ring Dang Doo" became immortal. Elmer V. Osborne had done some singing in Missouri, so he and two other guys formed the Grabass Trio, and their songs became a feature performance of the wardroom and the ship's entertainment.

Any occasion from promotions to birthdays gave a plausible excuse for a party, which became the setting for this "all-star" show. One of its big-time hits was the terpsichorean pursuits of those famous danseuses "Maud and Mabel" as portrayed by Parsons and Knute, complete with lipstick and stuffed bras. They refused to wear the girdles.

Refreshments at these affairs always consisted of ice cream, Coke, and cake. We even put the show "on the road," playing for affairs in the torpedo and bomber ready rooms. Those guys appreciated the entertainment break and always asked for an encore. In days to come, on the wide-open spaces of the Pacific where the sole source of entertainment was watching carrier takeoffs and landings or listening to Guy Robertson's donated phonograph playing his record collection, these shows—simple as they were—lifted morale and spirit.

Hawaii

- 44 -

After voyage repairs and loading urgently needed cargo for the war zone, the *Franklin* left San Diego and pointed her bow westward, accompanied by the three destroyers and the cruiser *Denver.* She made a fast voyage to Pearl Harbor without air patrol and entered the winding channel to Ford Island on June 5. Without the air patrol, we were all required to stand watches around the clock on the second deck for a very grim, sleepless few days.

We finally made it, and most of us saw for the first time the historic battleground of December 7, 1941. The USS *Franklin*, her camouflage paint job the fashion of the day, moved slowly into Pearl Harbor, gliding past the partially submerged hull of the USS *Arizona.* This was the Pearl Harbor we had heard and read about. We were at the double estuary of the Pearl River, called "Wai Momi" (Pearl Waters) by the Hawaiians. We moved past the waters where the *Utah, Arizona,* and the *Oklahoma*—once proud ships—were now rusting hulks after being bombed during the Japanese attack.

All hands who were not on duty lined the edge of the port flight deck and hangar deck as we passed, viewing these grim reminders, now rusty and decaying. The experience reconfirmed why we were headed to the Pacific to hunt down and destroy the enemy who had declared war on the United States. Two thousand three hundred eighty-eight Americans died during that early morning sneak attack—the Japanese had struck and escaped without encountering a counterattack, losing fewer than one hundred men. "Remember Pearl Harbor" had become a rallying cry across the United States, and as we not only viewed the damaged ships but also thought about the lives lost, I realized our job that lay ahead was more than justified.

A small navy band played "Aloha" as our ship tied up to the Ford Island dock; I have a vivid memory of the musicians in their summer whites playing their instruments at the dock's edge. The band's duty was to welcome incoming ships. Our duty was to fulfill our combat training. It was a very stirring, emotional, and patriotic moment.

Our planes were unloaded at Ford Island and flown to NAS Puunene, Maui. We were in Hawaii for temporary duty, on the Pacific outskirts of the conflict to continue honing our skills and await orders. We would be at Puunene for an indeterminate period. If you believed rumors, scuttlebutt had it that other groups remained from one to three months before being shipped out. Expecting to stay at least a month, I sent all my good clothes to the base laundry.

Maui has a most interesting topography. The pinched waist of the island is a lush valley, the ground bright red from iron oxidization, the soil composed of volcanic ash, rotted vegetation, crumbling lava, sand, and dirt deposited hundreds of years ago, stretching from seashore to seashore. Mountain crests tower on either side of the valley. Our airstrip and compound were carved out of a huge pineapple plantation.

We flew every day, weather permitting, sometimes playfully in and out of the bulbous, tail, or cumulous cloud formations between many daily periods of rain. Our formation flew parallel to the shore at three hundred feet, four hundred yards out from a gargantuan rock formation that descended into the sea, its waterfall cascading over the rocks, plunging into the ocean. One day McGraw commandeered a carry-all vehicle, and a group of us from the first two divisions went up to look at the extinct volcano Mount Haleakala, ten thousand feet up. Another day, we drove to the beach and swam in the heavy surf while we had time out due to a frontal system going through that had cancelled flight operations. Squadron softball games were organized. All in all, we were having a good time.

As junior officers, we had no concept of the current status of the war other than information that drifted down, nor did we have any idea of plans for our air group. Just seven days after we arrived, we returned to Ford Island to board the *Franklin* as she left Pearl, escorted by the new cruiser *Denver* and the destroyers *Twiggs and Leasy*, plus two other destroyers, all of which then stood out to sea. All my good clothes unfinished at the laundry were left behind.

When the ship was well clear of the harbor, Commander Day—Big Ben's executive officer—spoke to all hands. "Gentlemen, on June 15, today, the amphibious forces will land the Second Marine Division and the Twenty-Seventh Army Division on the Japanese island of Saipan in the Mariana group. The landings will be supported by the Seventh United States Fleet under Vice Admiral Kinkaid.

"The Fifth Fleet, Vice Admiral Spruance, consisting of carriers and battleships in Task Force Fifty-Eight, will operate between Saipan and the Philippines, the direction from which the Japanese are expected to counterattack. The First Carrier Task Force—of which the *Franklin* will be a unit—will cover the landings and destroy the Imperial Japanese fleet if the opportunity presents itself. One group of fast carriers will neutralize by bombing the Bonin Islands of Iwo Jima and Chichijima, from which the Japanese might send air strength into the Marianas.

"At last report, an enemy concentration of six battleships, five carriers, twelve cruisers, and thirty destroyers was assembled in the Philippines and has been sighted by our submarines moving into the Philippine Sea. Make no mistake. We think the Japanese are going to come out and fight this time. We are going to be ready for them. The *Franklin*, with her escorts, will remain in reserve in the Eniwetok area as reinforcements until called upon. This is it."

Commander Day's announcement explained the abruptness of our departure. Our destination was clear—combat. We were to join Adm. Marc Mitscher's Task Force Fifty-Eight. Our tropical training vacation was over. We were honest-to-goodness on our way to war.

USS Franklin in the Pacific

A Letter Home

- 45 -

On June 13, 1944, less than a month away from combat, I sent this letter to my parents, believing they would want to share the excitement of the precision involved with our wartime carrier operations and that hearing from me and knowing what my thoughts were would make them feel they were a part of my everyday flying life. I wanted them to know how much I appreciated their support all through my training. I was twenty-two years old and about to enter the Pacific combat zone as part of Adm. Marc Mitscher's Task Force Fifty-Eight. Here's what my letter said.

Dear Mom and Dad,

Here's something I wrote for you that will give you an idea of what happens on the carrier.

"Fighter pilots, man your ready room," said the loud speaker that had fast become all too familiar and annoying the past months aboard ship. In response to its uncompromising demands, the junior officers in the JO bunk room of Fighting Thirteen hastened to lay up to their air-conditioned sanctuary. Across the hangar deck, up the ladder, and through the island structure to ready room number 1 we went, where the tireless record player sang its repertoire of popular and classical music.

A practice group attack was in the offing, and the pilots jotted down pertinent data on their navigation plotting boards—ship's course and speed, our course away from the ship and the intercept course back and intercept time, all drawn in with pencil—before manning the planes on the flight deck. Some relaxed in the comfortable ready room chairs, awaiting their flight command. A few games of gin rummy broke out. Last-minute cigarettes were lit. Parachute harnesses were adjusted and Mae Wests examined for safety. The skipper gave the boys a few last-minute warnings of caution and explained the details of the attack.

Routine as these events had become, I still felt an air of anticipation just as I had the day I made my first carrier landing.

Having brought my plotting board up to date, I took a few drags on my cigarette. Then the order came. "Number 1 ready room, pilots, man your planes!" We grabbed our gear and scrambled to the flight deck and our taut-looking fighters. All orders were carried out "on the double" from this point on, and we ran aft on the deck and climbed onto the wings of our respective planes. The torpedo and dive-bomber pilots and crews were now running to their planes, which were spotted aft the fighters.

I slid my plotting board into its sheath, hung my oxygen mask on the gunsight, and climbed into the cockpit, snapping my parachute on with the aid of my plane captain. Then came the safety belt and shoulder straps, which bound me into the plane with a positive snap. The plane captain attached my radio cord as I ran through the checklist—fuel selector, mixture, tabs, cowl flaps, low pitch, and the rest of the list. She was all set to turn over—the bullhorn called, "Stand by to start engines of all fighters," as I primed the 2000 "horses," which were waiting my cue . . . fuel pump on, hand on the starter, get set to put the mixture in auto rich, magneto switch on—"Stand clear of propellers"— there's the all-clear signal from my plane captain . . . just a few seconds—"Start engines," and with that, I started the three blades turning.

Auto right . . . she's caught . . . retard the throttle a little—give it a chance. OK, sounds good. I'm number eight to take off, won't be long now—there goes the skipper, Robby, George, O'Donnell. We're next, all set to taxi into position. Spread those wings—locked— clasps down. Mac's up; go ahead, Smitty. Brooksie is set; he's got the flag. Takeoff position. Hold the brakes and ease the coal to her . . . I'm ready, give me the checkered flag. Red—got it—tail up, straight as a die down the deck, easy, airborne—gentle bank right—wheels up.

This is just a kind of peek at my thoughts while we are operating on the carrier. I thought I might explain operations to you somewhat and bring me a little closer to you at home. How does it sound? It's authentic on the factual side but a little amateurish from a literary standpoint!

Don't worry about me. Everything is OK, and I'm very careful.

Lots of love,
Bob

My parents were immensely proud of my achievement while terrified of the possibility that they might lose their only child. They keep all my correspondence in an old breakfront desk. I found this letter after they both had died, and I inherited their desk.

Part Five

The Pacific Theater

Our Division in the air

Destination: Eniwetok

- 46 -

One of the factors that strongly influenced the final decision to concentrate on the central Pacific and head for the Marianas was that the new B-29—the Superfortress bomber with a radius of 1,500 nautical miles and the capability of carrying 10,000 pounds of bombs— would need bases from which to attack Japan. With the Marianas secured, this powerful new bomber could reach the mainland of Japan. There was strong belief among the Combined Chiefs of Staff that Japan could be brought to surrender without an invasion and more loss of American lives.

Admiral Nimitz hesitantly agreed with MacArthur during a July 1944 conference in Hawaii, mediated by President Roosevelt, that an American invasion of the Philippines was a military necessity. Sights were zeroed in on the Marianas, a decision that set the stage, unbeknownst to them, for the Battle of the Philippine Sea or the Great Marianas Turkey Shoot.

As we headed for Eniwetok, there was an ice cream party in the ready room, and our newly formed band gave a still not finely tuned performance. Our jam session was held before a captive, enthusiastic audience—an audience not yet fully realizing how all our lives would change in a very short time.

At June 22, 1840, the *Franklin* crossed the equator, steaming west. That event called for the time-honored traditional crossing celebration. No one is really sure when the line-crossing ceremony Order of Neptune came about—a ritual that dates back at least four hundred years in Western seafaring. The ceremony observes a mariner's transformation from slimy pollywog—a seaman who hasn't crossed the equator—to a trusty shellback, also referred to as a son or daughter of Neptune. It was a test of seaworthiness for all sailors. King Neptune, a sailor who has crossed the equator many times, is surrounded by his shellback court to initiate the new pollywogs to pay proper homage to the god of the sea.

Our mission did not allow the usual grand festivity for this ritual as many on board had crossed the line before, but it was still held on a small scale. It was a fun occasion as I, among other first crossers, was transformed from a mere pollywog to a trusty shellback. It was another step in building camaraderie among the seafaring crew.

We proceeded to Eniwetok, and one hot afternoon, we slid into the harbor past the coral atoll, which had been devastated by our bombs only four months before. The palm trees looked like telephone poles that had been uprooted, splintered, and then inverted into the ground with great force. Not one blade of grass was visible on the ground. On shore, there were only coral, sand, and Quonset huts blistering under the sky that held off a blazing sun beating down with unmerciful constant heat.

Hardly a week after entering the circular lagoon of Eniwetok, orders arrived to proceed to rendezvous with Adm. Ralph Davison's Task Group 58.2 and head for Iwo Jima. We would be joining the *Wasp* and the light carriers *Monterey* and *Cabot,* escorted by the cruisers *Boston, Canberra,* and *San Juan,* with nine destroyers in the screen. The day we left the atoll, the ship hoisted the Foxtrot flag, signaling the beginning of flight operations.

Much of the operating structure of a navy squadron was organized around the pilots who had collateral jobs. Johnny Johnson and I, members of the flight department, were responsible for monitoring the fighter's carrier landings. When not in a combat zone, we stood on the LSO platform behind Casey and Dan, in front of the canvas wind barrier, and took notes on Casey's comments, later posting them in the ready room. A canvas laced on a pipe frame behind him protected Casey from the wind across the fir-planked deck—the rig included a "circus" net hung outboard of the ship over the water and slightly below the LSO platform, into which we could dive in case of an errant fighter plane landing.

When I didn't have LSO duty, I watched flight operations from the island or the catwalk at the edge of the deck, always fascinated by the drama, riveted by the superb coordination between men and machines, the incoming plane catching a wire, two deckhands sliding on kneepads under the tai, yanking the plane's hook from the cable while the fly three officer gave hand signals to the pilot to retract the hook. Now a plane director guided the fighter to a taxi spot while the next plane came right behind into the groove. Cables snapped up into place for the landing, the barriers banged up into position.

There was nothing as captivating as watching a navy aviator bring his plane aboard, entrusting himself and his plane to the trained and skilled hands of the ground crew. Stakes had now become not just practice. This was real. Errors could be too huge to imagine. We all kept in mind that Japan had not lost a war since 1592, and they never gave up.

Kelly

- 47 -

At 1214 hours on July 1, a great tragedy struck Fighting Thirteen with a suddenness that made even the most hard boiled of the squadron sober and sorrowful. While returning from an antisub patrol four days before first combat, Kelly was making a landing approach when, suddenly, his Hellcat went into a violent spin and crashed into the sea, breaking in two like a dry cigar just in the back of the cockpit. The plane disappeared in one minute—Kelly never made it out. The crew, stunned and distraught, still continued their job of bringing in the rest of the planes, making sure that all remaining aviators came in safely.

I was standing on the port catwalk. Word quickly spread that it was Lt. Clarence "Kelly" Blair, our executive officer. The emotional impact was shattering.

Members of the squadron went directly to the ready room as soon as all the fighters had landed, and we just slumped into our chairs, no one saying a word. Several of our enlisted men positioned themselves outside the two entrances to discreetly deflect any sympathizers while we held a closed-door meeting. In about ten minutes, the skipper entered the room and asked Stilwill to get any pilots remaining on the flight deck below. The skipper and Kelly had been close, the only two officers in the squadron who shared a bond of being graduates of the Naval Academy at Annapolis.

After we had assembled, the skipper spoke to us simply and right to the point. He addressed us, saying, "Boys, we have all, the fifty-five of us, lived together, worked together, and played together in each other's company and no others since the latter part of October 1943. Eight months together, we all knew Kelly and Tessie, his wife, intimately. We attended many parties together. Our squadron has had a lot of luck so far—well, our luck ran out today, and Kelly is gone."

I felt my emotions rush and almost overpower me. My throat constricted—I was afraid I was going to burst into tears.

The skipper continued, "He was a 4.0 naval officer and a grand guy. I'll miss him—you'll miss him, but we must go on. Don't let this thing get you down, boys. Let this be a grim lesson to you. Kelly wrapped the plane up in a tight turn. He died trying to make our squadron look good. He wouldn't go starboard of the island and attempted to come aboard in too tight a turn. Don't let it bother you. Keep right in there, making your normal approaches. You know the job we have to do on the fourth. You know how Kelly wanted to be there with us. Well, he will be. He'll be flying right along with us, then and always. I firmly believe that he is still a part of Fightin' Thirteen. That's all I have to say."

No one spoke. Frank Timmes, from Long Island with two Zeros to his credit at Guadalcanal, and Magnusson, the oldest fighter pilot in our group, turned to us and broke our silence, saying, "Let's get some chow."

At its lowest ebb, the squadron stood. The only sound was the muffled scrape of shoes against the steel ready room deck. We silently headed for the wardroom and lunch.

Not a word was spoken at the tables in the wardroom. There was not the usual joking, and the mess boys who normally tried to hurry everyone along stood at a respectful quiet distance for some time while eight of us sat and mourned our dead shipmate in manly fashion, silently and in company of one another.

Our thoughts turned to pretty Tessie at home in Rhode Island, still blissfully ignorant of the shock and sorrow she would bear in a few days with the arrival of that dreaded telegram. "The Navy Department regrets to inform you . . ."

Ready For Battle

- 48 -

The Great Marianas Turkey Shoot changed our expectations. We were thrust into combat earlier than expected because of that wild event near Guam, Saipan, and Tinian. Adm. Marc Mitscher launched two hundred aircraft from two hundred miles out, taking the Japanese by surprise and destroying over fifty of their planes both on the ground and in the air. It became the largest carrier-to-carrier battle in history, during which Japan lost the bulk of its carriers and would never recover.

Now it was our turn. Sixteen navy Hellcats, each armed with six rockets attached to the firing rails on the underside of the wings and six .50-caliber machine guns, were scheduled for takeoff from the *Franklin* at 0430, Pacific time, on July 4, 1944. A predawn fighter sweep—this was the first serious, life-threatening combat for our squadron. Our target was Iwo Jima, an eight-square-mile island in the Volcano, an archipelago, and the Bonin Islands, which were only six hundred miles south of Tokyo.

This Independence Day strike may have been timed as a patriotic ploy, but in reality, Admiral Nimitz felt it was strategically essential to neutralize the airfield, keeping the Japanese fighters inoperable. It didn't hurt that the fireworks we were about to create would be a great morale booster for "the war effort" at home. Adm. Jocko Clark had sent fighters into Iwo the afternoon before, which meant we would be expected by the Japanese.

The United States fleet was now on a Pacific Ocean rampage as army and marine troops invaded and advanced island by island across the Pacific toward Japan. Iwo's strategic value to the Japanese was its location as an interceptor flight base. The primary mission of the sweep was to tear up the runways, destroy aircraft in the air and on the ground, and hit antiaircraft installations. Any and all targets of opportunity were in our sights.

Our knowledge of the target area was excellent. We had spent several hours studying the topography, installations, runways, and general layout of the island supplied by navy intelligence and given to us by Lt. George Heinrich, VF-13's air combat intelligence officer. After being awakened at 0330, those of us scheduled to fly had breakfast in the officer's wardroom and then gathered in the ready room, where we had a final briefing on the day's overall operation, specifically on the predawn flight.

Each day preceding this first combat experience seemed to grow shorter to me. My anxiety kept building. What would we encounter? How skilled would the enemy fighters and their Zero planes be? What would happen if I was shot down and landed in enemy territory? How vulnerable would we be? Most of us had never been shot at before—at least not for real. Now we would be facing an enemy whose mission was to kill us. *Stay calm, Bob.* It was better to put all these negative thoughts out of my mind.

The seats in the Hellcats were adjustable, up or down. I always liked to fly with my seat all the way up for the best visibility, to be on top of what I was doing. It suddenly dawned on me that I would be a clear target sitting up so high and so visible. Maybe I should lower my seat?

What shoes should I wear? The shoe issue for me was a superstition, and later, it became a compulsive obsession that took on a life-and-death meaning of its own to me. I had visions of being shot down over the ocean while wearing ankle-high sturdy, heavy, tightly laced Marine combat boots; and if I parachuted into the water or made a water landing, I'd be wasting precious survival time in the water getting those damn heavy laced boots off. The choice was either the boots or brown leather oxfords with a couple of eyelets for laces, easy to kick off in the water, but should I land in rough jungle growth, they would be totally inadequate. How far could I hike in rough jungle terrain in a pair of flimsy oxfords? This morning, because Iwo was a small island, the chance of being downed in the water was much more likely than on land. I wore the oxfords.

A last check of my gear, and I was ready. I slid my Mae West over my head; snapped the hooks; adjusted my parachute harness and survival pack; secured my .38-caliber pistol in its holster; belted on my canteen, hunting knife, and machete; and went over the pencil notes on my plotting board, making certain that the coordinates for the ship's course and position on return were correct. I wrapped my red bandanna into a single strand and tied it around my neck, knotted in the back, and pulled on my white cloth helmet with my oxygen mask attached. I wore the custom goggles I had bought in San Diego, and I had a scary little wooden cannibal image from some tourist shop pinned on the back of my helmet to frighten off any Japanese pilot trying to come at me from behind.

We all wore dog tags, an oval metal chip about the size of a fifty-cent piece attached to a chain with name, navy serial number (I've never forgotten mine—301138), and blood type stamped in the metal. Most guys wore theirs on a long loose chain. I wore mine on a tight neck chain, my small resistance to regimentation. I never wanted to be like everyone else.

My great-aunt Fanny, my maternal grandfather Robert Waller's sister who lived in Minneapolis, had sent me a Saint Christopher medal—his name signifying "one who carries Christ." He is the patron saint of travelers and is invoked in storms, tempests, and plagues. Aunt Fanny married a Catholic, the only person in her English, Scottish, part-Irish Protestant family who bravely bolted from her family ranks. I never knew that full family story, but it must have been a beauty. Fanny, like her Canadian brother, was bright, feisty, and courageous. I loved her and felt her love coming to me through the medal, which even my staunchly anti-Catholic parents wouldn't object to. I wired it onto my neck chain with the dog tags. If Saint Christopher had some power, Catholic or not, it was OK with me. Maybe he would be especially potent on fighter sweeps.

A confirmed Episcopalian, I received *A Prayer Book for Soldiers and Sailors* with this inscription: "May God guide, sustain, and protect you in the service of your country and bring you safely home. Your friend and rector, Ernest E. Piper, St. Matthias, Detroit." He also sent me a medal inscribed, "Christ died for thee." On the back was its title, "The Church War Medal." It had two Maltese crosses imprinted above the title. I attached it along with Saint Christopher to my dog tag chain. I felt well cared for.

A few last instructions from Cap Coleman, and we were ready. "Number 1 ready room, pilots, man your planes" came over the squawk box, and we were out on the catwalk and up the ladder to the flight deck, hurrying through the darkness to our planes, which were spotted mid-deck. We never knew which plane would be ours to fly. One of the skipper's privileges of rank was he always flew the same Hellcat—number 1.

The darkened ship turned into the wind, getting the headwind blowing down the flight deck bow to stern. No lights were permitted on planes or the ship. Even though the moon was out, it seemed awfully dark to me. I climbed onto the port wing using the steps and handholds built into the fuselage, slid my plotting board into its sheath under the instrument panel, climbed over the edge, and lowered myself into the cockpit.

Going through the preflight checklist, my mind as dark as the night, I wondered if I would be lucky. I told myself I had the courage, and I was sure I had the skill, or I wouldn't be sitting in this cockpit, on this carrier, somewhere in the dark Pacific Ocean, ready for takeoff. I needed all the strength of mind I could bring to this morning so I would not self-destruct. Now I had to measure up to my own expectations and the navy's.

The bullhorn blasted over the dark deck. "Stand by to start engines of all fighters!" I primed the engine, fuel pump on, hand on the starter, mixture in auto rich, magneto switch on. "Stand clear of propellers." It was the plane captain's all clear. "Start engines." I'm number eight— set to taxi into position. Excited? Yes. Nervous? You bet. Focused? Damned right.

0430, Pacific Time, July 4

- 49 -

Because of some mix-up or delay, the second group of eight fighters never joined us, much to our skipper's anger, which was quite palpable in his voice. It was a bad start as we were now behind schedule. We headed for Iwo Jima without them. Eight planes flew in close formation just above the water, blue-black fighters barely visible except for each plane's pale blue exhaust flame, cloaked in the secrecy of the night, with no running lights allowed. We skimmed the water for as long as possible to avoid detection by Japanese radar—it was a classic navy predawn fighter sweep to neutralize the island's enemy airfield.

Early light began to color the sky with gold on the horizon, which I kept scanning for the shape of the island. As we climbed to push-over altitude to begin our first firing dive, the unmistakable shape of Mount Suribachi gradually began to emerge through the morning gloom, defining our target. In the distance, fighters from the carrier *Wasp* arrived over the target moments before we did and were making their runs on the airstrip. We couldn't see them, but we knew they were there because of the streaming barrage of antiaircraft tracer fire spewing up from the island, fire we would soon be plunging through.

Antiaircraft fire, known as AA (for *ack-ack*), whether shot from Japanese naval vessels or from camouflaged gun emplacements with its hail of bullets and shells, was deadly. A shell exploding near a plane or formation could shred metal, rip off a wing, or shatter a propeller. Small-caliber rounds could tattoo the skin of our planes and engines. The Hellcat's radial power plant, the big eighteen-cylinder, double-bank engine, was a large bull's-eye for AA—pilots were protected by the plane's strong cockpit armor plate.

As violent as the scene was, it was also was strangely beautiful, almost surreal. I had a sudden time travel back, thinking how much the brilliant explosions reminded me of the Fourth of July firework shows my parents took me to when I was a boy.

We reached ten thousand feet and started jinking—banking severely left and right. After the skipper's division began its run, we started our firing run, nosing over in loose formation, planes spread out. With my plane aimed at the ground, I could see the runway, but what I was most conscious of were the big blobs of black AA smoke we were diving through. They seemed to be coming straight at me. Down, down we went, building up tremendous speed, now going through gray smoke spirals as smaller AA guns picked us up.

At one thousand feet, I fired two rockets, saw them zoom toward the runway, and began my pullout, g-forces pulling the skin of my face down, vapor trails streaking up to the wing roots as the plane went through a high-speed stall. Banking the plane violently left and right to present the most difficult target for ack-ack as possible, I sensed rather than saw the reddish-brown volcanic earth airfield. I sped over it low, four hundred feet, heading away from the island, out over the water. Circling left and up, I intercepted Brooks to join him for the next run. Instruments installed on some of the fighters that day recorded speeds of over five hundred knots in those dives, almost unheard-of speed at that time.

We continued climbing around Iwo to regain altitude for another rocket run. During the briefing, the skipper had said we would make two runs, so this was the last ride down Tracer Hill, which was OK with me. Over we went again, released our rockets, and pulled out— eight Hellcats still intact.

My earphones crackled. It was the skipper. "We'll make one more run."

I said to myself, "You said two, damn it!" Hearing anything on the radio under these circumstances was unusual. Strict radio silence was always stressed, no unnecessary chatter. So back up we went for a third run.

As we got into position, about to nose over, instinct—or was it Providence?—made me glance over my left shoulder. I saw four planes coming down behind us. I was startled. My first thought was they were probably our guys, maybe the ones who had missed the rendezvous after our takeoff. I hoped they were our guys sliding in to catch up behind us. The process of one's action and reaction during a moment like that can be measured in fractions of seconds. Recalling this, even fractions seem indolent, lazy.

The first plane behind me opened fire. This was red alert. These were not friends.

I'm Hit

- 50 -

The planes were Zeros, each painted mustard gray with a rust-red cowling and nose cone—red Japanese "meatballs" prominently displayed on the wings and fuselage. I was the fourth man in our division, meaning the first exposed target. The Zero's twenty-millimeter rounds of tracers went streaming by and then whack!

My plane jolted heavily upon impact. The stick banged sideways hard, out of my grip, and smacked my thigh. A shell had hit my starboard wing about eight feet outboard, entered the upper wing surface, and exploded, causing a seven-inch diameter entry hole. Brooks, ahead and to my left, suddenly filled my windscreen. He had banked hard right to avoid being hit. I yanked the stick to right as hard and fast as I could to avoid a midair collision. Seconds later, I banked left to get out of his way.

As swiftly and silently as the Japanese had appeared, they disappeared—not a trace of them. Also, there was no trace of Brooks. He had rolled over and down back into his firing run. I pressed the transmit button and hollered into the mike in my oxygen mask, "Brooksie, Brooksie, I'm hit! I'm hit!" I said it as if he could help me.

Suddenly, I felt completely alone. Numbed and momentarily in shock, I cruised down in a shallow dive, silently praying not to be shot at again. I was like a wounded bird on the lookout for the rescue submarine while thinking I might have to make a water landing and, with luck, would be picked up by the rescue sub.

In our preflight briefing, we were told that the rescue submarine would be on station on the far side of the island. Johnny Johnson found it. Or should I say it found him in his life raft after he was shot down. It's amazing what flashes through your mind in moments of survival. My superstitious shoe theory came to the front of my brain. At least I was wearing my good old oxfords and so much for the help of the scary little cannibal image on the back of my helmet keeping the enemy at bay.

As I leveled off about a one hundred feet above the water, I realized several things. My plane was very unstable. The exploding shell had severed the cable to the right aileron, making it useless. When the wind caught the aileron, it would flip up or down, causing the plane to bank sharply, unexpectedly, and I had to cross controls—stabilize my lateral position by making the left aileron do what the mindless right aileron was doing. Suddenly directly ahead of me, a Japanese Zero spiraled down past me, one wheel lowered, looking surreal, prop windmilling—no pilot was visible. I watched the plane as it crashed into the sea.

The next thing I realized was that I couldn't see any sign of the rescue sub. At the same moment, a formation of our torpedo bombers was heading away from the island, so I figured that my best bet was to follow them. By now, I had developed a technique for keeping my plane flyable. By making wide, shallow turns to the left and forward, I was able to keep the maverick fighter under control, and I tagged along at the rear of the bomber formation, not knowing if they were VT-13's and homing on the *Franklin* or VT-5's, going back to the *Wasp*. It didn't matter to me. They were friendly, and at the moment, I needed friends badly.

I flew like some crazy bird going around and around in circles until our odd armada arrived over the fleet and *CV-13*. Now I was almost home. Having decided a carrier landing was impossible, with the plane being too fickle, I climbed to five thousand feet, positioning myself ahead of the lead destroyer in the task group. I unplugged the radio cord to my helmet, unsnapped my seat belt, cranked open the canopy, throttled back, lowered the flaps to slow the plane, and got ready for a bailout. To my great surprise, the plane suddenly became almost stable, if a one-aileron fighter could be called stable.

A glance at the fuel gauge showed I had plenty of fuel left, so I made a decision. I closed the canopy, fastened my seat belt, plugged in the radio jack, and with flaps down descended toward the *Franklin*. I worked my way into the landing pattern and started going through the emergency landing procedure, flying past Casey, the landing signal officer, and blipping the engine by rapidly moving the throttle back and forth in short thrusts. I radioed my emergency to the carrier, whose call sign was Buick, a word difficult for the Japanese to pronounce, thinking my message would get to the LSO. I continued working my way between the planes that were making their own scheduled approach while blipping my engine as I flew past the port side of the ship.

Circling with my plane still performing erratically, I came around on my approach into the groove, just above stalling speed, when I saw an SB2C Helldiver coming in from my left, both of us converging simultaneously on the flight deck. I couldn't wrap it up (turn hard) to avoid him, so I pushed right rudder, holding the plane as level and steady as I could. I skidded right less than one hundred feet above the water and headed for the starboard side of the ship's superstructure while the dive-bomber ducked down under the fantail of the ship, beneath the stern of the carrier, just above the water and skittered off beneath me to my right somewhere, clearing the area.

It was a court-martial offense to fly through the exhaust of the ship's engines because the turbulent, invisible heat was strong enough to flip a plane into the water. I held my breath and didn't pass through the deadly zone. I felt light headed. I must have been breathing in panic-induced short gasps, not taking in enough oxygen. Another circle around the ship, and the stage was now to myself—I was in the final turn for landing. My approach was good, and I got the LSO's cut signal and brought my wounded bird down.

After I caught a wire, for a split second, I felt as though I would collapse in my seat, mind, body tension, and adrenaline all suddenly released. My hook was disengaged by the deck crew while the deck officer was waving crazily for me to clear the way for the next plane. The barrier banged down. I shot forward with a strong burst of throttle out of the critical landing space, opened the cowl flaps to cool the hot engine, and followed the lane director's taxi signals past two firefighters in asbestos suits standing next to the island.

My episode had delayed the landing of two bomber groups who were circling and waiting, all the while using up precious fuel. What I didn't know was that I had a rocket hung up under one of the wings of my plane, and a twelve-inch hole blasted out of the leading edge of the right wing. I don't know why the rocket didn't fire. Perhaps the connection to the firing mechanism was fouled. The ship had anticipated that the rocket might fire off when I landed, making my plane a live explosion.

Commander Kibbe, skipper of VF-13 who was flying the Helldiver that had gone under me on my approach, came by our ready room later and said, "I didn't know you had an emergency landing. God, I'm sorry I endangered your approach." That guy did have class.

We didn't lose any pilots on the mission, but tragically, Dave James crashed on deck so hard on his return landing that he sustained a severe head injury that deemed him no longer able to fly. Johnny Johnson, who was shot down and rescued in his rubber raft at sea, spent the next six weeks on the rescue submarine. Jimmie Carpenter's engine was pretty shot up, but he had just enough cylinders undamaged to maintain power and landed with oil splattered all over his windshield, posing a severe visibility problem. I flew two more hops over Iwo Jima that same day, tired and somewhat shaken but thankful to be alive.

All in all, four enemy aircraft were destroyed in the air and fourteen on the ground, plus four merchant vessels destroyed along with three others damaged. We were all dog tired. Happy Fourth of July. This was just the beginning.

Guam Invasion

- 51 -

From Iwo, we were hustled directly to Guam, which was one of the four major Japanese bases in the Marianas. Saipan, the main base, was being wrest from the Japanese by army and marine soldiers. Rota, Tinian, and Guam still remained. Our mission was to soften them up for the forces that were scheduled to land.

We arrived off the northeast coast of the island on the morning of July 6. That afternoon, we blasted the Japanese shore installations, sixteen fighter pilots thundering over the enemy's major positions, pouring destruction by starting dozens of fires, silencing their guns, and blasting any buildings of importance. Battleships and cruisers pounded relentless shell after shell onto Guam day after day. The air-sea bombardment was one of the most intense operations to date in the Pacific war.

The takeover of Guam was our mission. The more the navy could inflict damage, both physically and structurally, as well as much demoralization of the enemy's mindset, the better it would be for the marine and army troops in the upcoming land invasion. A plan of simultaneous bombing and strafing from the air along with the ship's gunfire at sea was tried for the first time. The ships limited their maximum ordinates of shell trajectory to 1,200 feet—pilots were required to pull out of their runs at 1,500 feet. It was a well-orchestrated effort—we wanted Guam.

We began flying three strikes a day, strafing with guns and rockets against the Japanese gun emplacements on the island. On one of the first hops, antiaircraft fire got Willie Grove just as he was starting his dive. He was hit in the wing, which caught fire. As Willie told it, he knew he had to get into the water and fast. Once in the water, he was out of the cockpit in thirty seconds, struggling to get out of his shoot pack and into his life raft.

It can be pointed out here that a navy pilot doesn't exactly carry a raft—he sits on it. The raft is compressed into a square about the size of a sofa cushion and is sandwiched between the parachute and seat cushion, fixed in place with straps and buttons. Extracting the raft is not exactly easy. It could be compared to a man trying to get rid of a horsefly in his briefs. Once you get past that wrestling match, you have to inflate it and get into the thing—a clumsy contraption to board at best. Finally, Willie removed his shoes, conquered the raft, and spent a long night in the dark sea on his inflatable.

Early the next morning, Air Group Thirteen's boss, Cmdr. Sunshine Howerton; Fighting Thirteen's skipper, Lt. Cmdr. Cap Coleman; Lt. Ted Hudson, Willie's roommate and squadron flight officer; and Ensign Cal Price accompanied an OS2U Kingfisher, along with two planes, plus a single pontoon observation plane to try to find and rescue Gove. They circled over the area believed to be where he went down as related the day before by Ensign Roger L'Estrange, who was in Will's division and the last to see him. On a second pass, Ted saw the wink of a bright light below. Willie was signaling from the raft with the mirror from his survival kit. Thank god for sunny days. Ted hand-signaled the skipper, and they dived toward Willie and began circling him. The Kingfisher pilot, Lt. Fred Rigdon, made a successful water landing, taxied over to Willie, hauled our guy aboard, and got the hell out of there.

Escorted by the four fighters, Rigdon flew back with Willie to his home base, landed in the water, and was hauled aboard the ship by crane—standard procedure. The cruiser was the *Boston*. Our rescued

Willie was a Walpole, Massachusetts, boy, so naturally, he was clothed, fed, and feted before sending him home to the *Franklin*.

We flew seventeen straight days, pounding Guam three flights a day against designated targets, with a break for sandwiches served in the ready room for lunch. There was little air opposition due to the losses the Japanese endured in the Philippine Sea battle and the Turkey Shoot. On July 21, our division flew with the skipper's division to cover the first wave of the invasion at 0830; we went in ahead of the advancing troop-laden landing craft, guns strafing, rockets firing, battleships and cruisers shelling. The busy landing crafts circled the transports, pulling alongside to load troops, and then darted away, heading for the beach.

All pilots of the task group were issued small cards—about 5" × 6"—that had grids printed on them of the shore area right up into the hills. Sections of this area were marked off and coded with letters and numbers. Strike coordinators flew on station for the invasion, directing strafing and bombing groups toward specific targets that had been relayed to them from the ground forces. We had our grids strapped to our thigh and could reference the area we were ordered to attack, pinpointing the exact target area we should hit ahead of advancing land troops.

While dangerous, I was kind of glad to be doing battle in the air. At that moment, it looked extremely dangerous to me, looking down on the ground troops.

Combat Air Patrol

- 52 -

We left Task Force 58.2 under the command of Adm. Marc Mitscher and became Task Force 38.4, now back under the command of Adm. Bull Halsey. The group consisted of two large carriers, Big Ben and the *Enterprise*; two medium-sized carriers, the *San Jacinto* and the *Belleau Wood*; one cruiser; and four destroyers.

Combat air patrol (CAP) was shared by all four fighter squadrons of the task group on a rotation basis. This became our flying "job." We would orbit the fleet at ten thousand to fifteen thousand feet, waiting for the fighter director officer to identify bogeys (enemy planes). If a target was spotted, he would vector the four-plane division with a buster, meaning bogeys were getting closer. This was usually a boring three-hour flight, which could last well over five hours.

We had no mission other than to remain on aerial standby. We flew in loose formation, adhering to a roughly rectangular pattern, alone with just our thoughts. The hours seemed endless; the flying was more than tedious. My muscles were knife-edge tense from being strapped into the cockpit in the same position for such long periods. Perspiration soaked my flying suit, and the sweat on my head lodged in my hair under the cloth helmet, becoming torturously uncomfortable. There was nothing glamorous about combat air patrol.

In contrast to the boredom was the glorious panorama I could look down from the air at the entire powerful fleet moving through the clear blue-green water. The ship's bows cut through the ocean, causing huge spraying white waves. Even though we were at war, there were times the sights of naval life at sea were majestic.

As the daily hours droned on, I found that my head itched mercilessly after an hour. My shoulders, tense from concentration and from a total lack of movement, would stab with burning pain. I found myself checking my watch frequently, almost like a kid waiting for the three o'clock school bell to ring, announcing class dismissal. I always wore my watch on my left wrist facedown so I could see the time without lifting my hand from the throttle, waiting for either a bogey or the end of our patrol. There were times I thought I didn't remember seeing Errol Flynn in his flying movies sweating and uncomfortable like this while in his goggles and helmet.

One welcome tension relief was an occasion when, after one extralong, five-hour duty, McGraw—our division leader, a combat-experienced dive-bomber pilot from the USS *Enterprise* in the early stages of the Pacific war—nosed over, and the four of us went plummeting down for no reason other than release pent-up energy on the carrier. It was an incredible, Errol Flynn–like thrill. As we pulled out of our "tension release" dive, throttles back, bleeding off speed, we closed up tight in an overlapping starboard echelon formation and flew past the ship out from the island superstructure. At that moment, we were navy fighter pilots fulfilling the high standards of the Navy Air Corps. We were not unlike a professional sports team exhibiting the best of the best and very proud at that.

The ship's main function was to bring planes home, landing safely and, at the same time, as quickly as possible. This responsibility was shared by the landing signal officer and his assistant, the flight deckhands, and the deck officers, all working together in finite synchronization. The air officer was an overall supervisor, referred to as the air boss, a great and well-deserved title. The helmsman and duty officer on watch were part of this large orchestration—their job was to be sure the ship's heading was accurately pointed toward the wind blowing across the floating runway. All of them shared a partnership in this most critical, extremely dangerous, and highly dramatic operation. The efficiency of getting planes back aboard had a number one priority—land the pilots safely. But it also had a corollary, which was to assure minimum gas consumption by the planes before they could land. During a large-scale flight operation with fighters, dive-bombers, and torpedo bombers, all consuming fuel, the efficiency of landing without wasted time was critical to the gas supply and the war effort.

After our tension release display, we passed the ship's superstructure to starboard, canopies open and locked, shoulder harness tight and locked, fuel selector on the fullest tank, engine turning 2,400 rpm, prop at low pitch. We dropped wheels, flaps, and tailhooks, each of us giving a thumbs-up to the other on visual inspection—Mac to Smitty, Smitty to Mac, Brooks to me, me to Brooks. Just past the ship, Mac broke left, and then each of us followed in turn, arcing out ahead and to the port side of the ship, positioning ourselves on the downwind leg, adjusting our height above the water by lining up the top of the ship's island with the far horizon, which gave us the proper height for this stage of the carrier landing pattern. The distance between planes was a matter of judgment as was most of the landing procedure.

Earlier in a noncombat zone, we conducted a landing drill—timed intervals between planes. Brooks landed ten seconds behind Smitty, and I landed ten seconds behind Brooks. Few equaled that interval. No one beat it. Competition was always present and always reigned high.

Because danger was omnipresent, the trust between pilots and their LSO was, and is, unique—a special bond like no other in aviation. The LSO was the judge and jury for landings. Never was the Navy Air Corps syllabus of precision flying more important or more demanding than in carrier landings. Planes were flown a few knots above stalling speed, nose high, a Hellcat's 2,500 pounds hanging on the propeller's 2,000 horsepower Pratt & Whitney radial engine. The LSO's visual signals with his arms extended, holding the signal paddles, arms straight out from his shoulders stated OK. Arms up, the plane was too high; arms low, you were too low. His left arm extended and right arm down at his side meant you were too fast to land—ease off a little power. Both paddles moving forward and back in a pulling motion called for more speed. If the pilot's approach was perfect, the LSO whipped his right paddle across his throat for a cut—the signal to chop throttle and land. Both arms above his head, waving, meant a wave off, whereupon the pilot slammed on full power, banking left and then right, paralleling the ship's course. Disobeying that signal was a court-martial offense because it could lead to disaster. The pilot might have made a perfect 4.0 approach, but the deck might have been foul—the barriers were not up, personnel were in the landing area, or the previous landed plane's tailhook was not yet disengaged. If the sea was rough and the ship pitching and rolling, pilots were not to use the deck as a visual reference but were expected to make a normal approach, concentrating on the LSO, whose job it was to judge the arrival of the plane with the undulating altitude of the flight deck.

Carrier landings demand flying excellence, which is what distinguishes the Navy Air Corps fleet operations. The price of a mistake in judgment was life threatening for all concerned. When a plane in the groove loses speed while in a high-risk altitude, it also loses lift, stalls, abruptly flips, and crashes into the water. Ensign Robert Martin, a replacement pilot and a new friend, died during such an approach, very much similar to Kelly's fate so many months earlier. That very danger was the essence, the challenge, of being the best you could be. Every navy aviator knows each landing he makes is challenging the laws of physics to land successfully on the aircraft carrier.

Being back aboard again after our watch was another victory. My neck and back muscles ached. They felt as though they were plugged into a thousand electrically charged needles. My spine felt like a reinforcement bar. My mouth was dry as sand while my cheeks and nose were redlined from the pressure of my green rubber oxygen mask. Salt crystals stained the back of my flight suit, giving my one-piece coveralls an oval off-white design. I pulled off my helmet and parachute harness, unsnapped my yellow Mae West, and unhitched my ammo belt.

Each pilot was personally fitted for his harness, a device whose heavy-duty clips snapped onto the rings of the parachute on the seat in the cockpit. The harness backpack was loaded with survival gear—dry food, fake chocolate, flares, and yellow stain containers to color the water, marking your position for rescue seekers if you bailed out or if you survived being shot down. It was all stuff the navy thought would be essential to survive for days in your inflatable rubber life raft or hack your way through the jungle. And of course, attached on top of the parachute was that very hard cushion—the life raft.

Life became a never-ending series of tests measuring your judgment by each safe return to the carrier, every proper takeoff, every successful catapult shot, not to mention being vigilant in the air. Almost all those summer evenings onboard in the Pacific were balmy, with steady, warm breezes pushing against our faces and khakis, reminding us that we were alive, which was to say full of no concepts other than hope. The huge ship powered through the ocean, heading into the night and toward another combat zone, which by definition was measured in air miles. How far could the enemy fly toward us versus how far were we able to fly toward them, make contact, and then still safely return to our base either on land or sea? Our ships in the task force were capable of speeds the enemy was still, for some reason, unaware of, thus allowing naval strategists the ploy of illusion. Our game was to portray to the Japanese a much larger carrier fleet than what actually existed. One could call it a street dealer's risky three-card monte on the sea.

One particular evening, my friend and I were standing together at the forward edge of the wood-planked flight deck on the 880-foot-long *Franklin*, trying to become as close to the future as our minds would allow. He and I speculated on our respective futures while we optimistically anticipated a soon ending to the war and what our new lives would be like when the war was over. As peaceful and hopeful as those moments were, the contrasting reality was extreme. Our air group flew with a mission to kill the enemy with bullets, bombs, rockets, and torpedoes who, in turn, would use the same firepower toward us. Yet the two of us dared to stand there on a balmy night in mutual confidence, soothed by the evening's tranquility, expecting a life filled with plans while living on a margin of hope.

The future of our fighter squadron's members argued against hope. The complement of the squadron was forty-eight pilots. We couldn't know during those balmy moments that fifteen of us would be killed or missing in action—almost one-third.

USS Franklin — Fighters warm up before takeoff on strike

Fun, Games, And Mail

- 53 -

Our lives onboard were defined by two conditions. We were either in a combat zone, minds on the alert for battle stations, entwined with the day's flight schedule, or not in a combat zone. There would be no CAP, no fighter sweeps, no flying fighter escort for dive-bombers and torpedo bombers, no tracer hills to brave—a welcome respite from carrier landings, takeoffs, and catapult shots. We had time to play bridge, poker, chess, or backgammon or just listen to records of the latest music and write letters home.

One of the intriguing subplots among ships in the Pacific was the exchange of movies. Who had what? It became a barter of "We saw that last month, castoff," or "We'll trade two Errol Flynns for one Betty Grable." Movies were shown when we were at anchor in some atoll, taking on supplies, making necessary repairs, or replenishing ammo and gas for the planes. Best of all, this was the time we finally would receive all our accumulated mail.

On evenings, the ship's band members, relieved from duty as stretcher bearers or ammo handlers, performed big band concerts on the hangar deck before the movies. Many of these guys were professional musicians, now enlisted men who came from the ranks of the Dorsey Brothers, Hal Kemp's orchestra, and other top bands. They were a great group led by Saxie Dowell, whose claim to fame were two classic pieces, "Three Little Fishies" and "Playmates."

Fierce, competitive, slam-bang volleyball games were played in the three-sided arena of the lowered forward elevator. We had a tiny space on the forecastle deck that served as a workout gym and also as the site of some "big-time" boxing slugfests. We boxed for fun, carrying on a competition we began while we were in Hawaii.

Mail was our only connection to the life we left behind. Letters from family, wives, girlfriends, fiancées, aunts and uncles, and friends were an instant transfusion of love, hope, and joy from the ugly reality we faced daily. Even the blandest greeting was heartwarming. Those thoughtful pieces of written connection gave us a private life in an otherwise very public one.

My mother wrote to my spirit, often sending meaningful poetry she had clipped from the *Detroit News* or copied from the pages of a book she was currently reading. She spoke from her heart while carefully hiding her fear and pain. My dad wrote once in a while. He was never very good at expressing his feelings—he was much better with frequent hugs and smiles, demonstrating his affection. He and my uncle Russ would spend hours together trying to figure out where the *Franklin* was by piecing together newspaper articles about the war in the Pacific on a chart they had made. It had almost become a weekly board game for them. Uncle Russ seldom wrote, sending his thoughts through my aunt Dolly, who kept me up to date on their life in Grand Rapids. My uncle Harold, a navy yeoman during WWI, would write now and then, his letters reflecting his personality—witty, cheerful, poetic, and understanding. He always cheered on my piano efforts at boogie-woogie and jazz, even though classical was his style.

The importance of letters to servicemen was clear to me early on before I left Detroit. I wrote to Johnny Carroll, my early flying buddy, while he was a cadet, eager to hear what life as a cadet was like from his viewpoint, cheering him on while casting myself in his role. In 1942, Johnny sent me *Wing Tips*, volume 1, a 4" × 6" Pensacola handbook of the Aviation Cadet Regiment of the United States Naval Reserve. It's a thorough discourse on what naval aviation cadets could expect and what was also expected of them. I treasured that gift from him.

Ed Armstrong, a fraternity brother I admired, became an army fighter pilot and was a faithful correspondent. His letters were full of both his fears and the thrills of flying.

Letters from Marge and Kay, both girlfriends at different times, kept my spirits up. I still longed to hear from Mary, but that prospect became dimmer with time.

The entertainment session parties were a highlight in our ready room. Our band formed the centerpiece of those parties with sing-along favorites like "Bye Bye Blackbird," "Everybody Loves My Baby," "I'm in Love with You, Honey," "I Wanted Wings," and many others. The band was augmented by the Grabass Trio with a repertoire that would make the Vienna Boys' Choir blush.

When Brooks made his five thousandth landing aboard Big Ben and McGraw his seven thousandth, both occasions called for wild, noisy celebrations. One of the loudest hoots was an evening when the ship picked up a Tokyo Rose radio broadcast from Japan and put it on the ship's speaker system. She announced in her soft, cooing, sultry, and very sexy voice that the *Franklin* had just been sunk. The parties were bawdy and robust—as hard as we fought the war, we partied with the same intensity. Our lives and our mental well-being depended on it.

Personal Log

- 54 -

The following is an excerpt from my personal log, which I began keeping when we left Norfolk, Virginia, heading west for combat. For security reasons, we were not supposed to keep any personal records, although a few of us did as I later learned.

There were three critical alerts broadcast over the ship's speakers— general quarters, battle stations, and torpedo defense. The *general quarters* command was for all hands to report to their workstations. This announcement was always preceded by the sound of the boatswain's pipe and then the announcement. "Now hear this. Now hear this. General quarters. General quarters."

Battle stations was the signal for imminent attack, and all hands hustled to their assigned station, often the same in all three instances, preceded by a banging gong. "Now hear this. Now hear this. Battle stations. All hands, man your battle stations."

Torpedo defense signaled an expected torpedo attack. A bugler on duty blew an odd tune signaling torpedo defense.

In more carefree moments, we made up these lyrics to sing with a tune. "Torpedo, torpedo, torpedo! Too late, too late, too late! Too late, too late, too late!"

Over Manila, our flight schedule was changed to code name Strike Able. I was scheduled for Strike Baker. Several bogeys had been shot down in the morning but none by our CAP.

At 1000, general quarters sounded. I ran up to the ready room from church and then onto the hangar deck, got into my gear, and manned my plane. We warmed up the planes and then were told to cut our engines. We returned to the ready room and had no sooner arrived when we were told to immediately man eight fighters on the deck for Strike Baker. I, along with the others, ran back to the planes and started the engines again, ready to take off.

Suddenly, there was a blast on the ship's horn, and the ship's guns began firing. I saw the skipper stop his engine and jump out of his plane. I looked up and saw puffs of AA fire, every gun in our fleet opening up fire.

Then I spotted a Japanese fighter at about one thousand feet coming right down toward the deck. Strapped in the cockpit, I frantically struggled out of my gear just as a bomb grazed the edge of the outboard elevator on the port side and exploded. Water splashed from the explosion and cascaded down on the deck. I was still struggling to get out of the cockpit.

A wave of smoke from the explosion went by as I ran like hell into a compartment on the deck and dived for cover with the men who were already there. There were several other bombs dropped. Luckily, all missed.

When the threat appeared to be over, we stood up in the bay, the skipper asking, "Everyone accounted for?"

With no time to spare, Brooks, Griffen, Smith, and I regrouped, manned planes, and took off. We remained on CAP from 1100 to 1500. Then Brooks, Griffen, and I landed on the deck of the *Belleau Wood*. Smith's engine had quit, forcing him to land in the water, where he was picked up by a destroyer. Brooks and I then took off from the *Belleau Wood* at 1545—another raid was on its way.

We circled at fifteen thousand feet but didn't get any contacts. *Enterprise* fighters had shot down twenty-one Japanese and turned back their raid. We landed on the *Franklin* at 1730. Strike Able shot down nineteen planes over Manila.

J. B. Johnson got two Japanese over Manila, but he was shot up himself. He couldn't make a water landing as suggested by the ship because his hood was jammed shut, and he was wounded in the arm. He landed aboard with no wheels and no flaps, but he safely made it "home."

Lieutenant Junior Grade Hudson of VT-13 and two enlisted men were killed by the bomb. Another VT pilot wasn't expected to live. Many of the crew were injured.

My visual recall of Doc Moy and stretcher bearers carrying the torpedo pilot facedown past my plane into a small bay on the starboard side as I was waiting to takeoff is fixed in my mind. The back of the pilot's shirt and pants were completely drenched in blood. Seeing his bloody body was another graphic reminder of the ugliness of war and killing. It was then, at that precise moment, I was reawakened to the horror of killing. Each of us, I'm certain, placed our faith in the belief that we would be spared, that nothing serious would happen to us, that our flying skill was abetted by God, and that luck would prevail.

Man Overboard

- 55 -

General quarters were manned by the nonflying personnel every morning while the ship was in a combat zone. The navy was always on the alert for a predawn attack on the task force. On this particular morning, dragged by fatigue, Lt. Cmdr. James T. Moy, MD, USN, headed toward his assigned time on the flight deck. Responding to general quarters, he turned right down the companionway after leaving his bunk room instead of making his usual left turn, which positioned him toward the direction of the port side of the carrier.

Conditioned to turn left when he reached the flight deck and head aft to the ship's island, which was his battle station, he did so inching through the blackest part of the predawn morning, believing he was on the starboard side of the ship. Instead, he was on the port side, groping through the moonless night, heading toward the ship's bow. One moment Doc Moy, our flight surgeon, was on the flight deck; the next moment, he stepped out into air off the port bow, sixty feet above sea level. Completing a full gainer in layout position and offering a short rather loud prayer—"Jesus Christ!"—he landed feet first, surfaced, and immediately swam away from the bow as fast as possible to avoid being sucked under by the big carrier pounding through the darkness.

It was about 0500 when the boatswain's pipe pierced the air through the speakers on the ship. A seaman bellowed, "Now hear this! Now hear this! Man overboard on the port side! Man overboard on the port side!"

I was awakened by the announcement and thought, *Some dumb sailor must have fallen off the ship*. And I went back to sleep.

All flight deck personnel were required to wear belt-type life preservers and carry a whistle attached to a cord. Needles, as we fondly called Doc Moy, was not wearing his preserver—naughty boy. But lucky for him, he had worn his whistle. A seaman on watch reported hearing loud, repeated toots coming from the water. Once the incredulous officers on watch realized the situation, the USS *Owen*, a destroyer, was dispatched and began a search for Doc.

A strong athlete, excellent swimmer, and well-trained diver, Lieutenant Commander Moy was able to stay afloat in the calm seas and was found by the destroyer several hours after taking the plunge, still strongly blowing his whistle. Later in the day, he was transferred by boatswain's chair back to Big Ben, where a large group of us—his seagoing medical practice—stood on the aft section of the flight deck port side and jeered him back aboard.

There was no end to the razzing over his predawn dip. A suicide motive came under serious discussion after his large losing gin rummy score was unearthed. Doc brushed it off, saying he had decided to test, with an early morning dip, if his former superb diving records still held. We were relieved he was back—so was he.

Fighting squadron Thirteen aboard USS *Franklin*

Splash One Tony

- 56 -

Three fighters were off to my right. Brooks, my section leader, was sixty feet away. We were in loose formation high over Manila Bay, throttles to the firewall, water injection switches on, cooling our Pratt & Whitney radial engines.

We were at twenty thousand feet, flying high cover for VF-13 dive-bombers who had begun their run on enemy ships in the harbor. The upper air was clean and clear, visibility excellent. Low clouds hugged the groundwaters and backwaters of the Philippine Island forests. Whatever planes the Japanese still had were being moved north in an attempt to preserve the dwindling number of planes they had left. We were now swarming over the enemy.

Four of us roared through the sky, hunting but tense. Mac's voice suddenly came in my earphones, saying, "Take him, Hungie." He had skillfully guided us to a position behind a Japanese Tony, now about one thousand feet ahead and two hundred to three hundred feet below. Flying in number four position, my main role was to act as the tail end guy and watch for attacks from the rear. I would be first to get shot at and most likely last to get shot at by an oncoming enemy plane. Mac had just given me a clear shot at the enemy—mine to take.

No prelude, just get the enemy plane in the orange gunsight ring glowing on the reflector glass on the windscreen and shoot. This was my singular moment after five months at sea and hours and hours of combat, now focused on this one instant. I was coming dead on the ass of the Japanese fighter who was unaware of the four Hellcats now swooping into his world.

I put my sights on the narrow body of the plane, instinct born of training. My gloved left hand held the throttle at the firewall, right hand on the stick, index finger curled over the red trigger of the six wing-mounted, .50-caliber machine guns.

The instant froze. My eyes held the enemy plane in the sight as I came roaring silently in my mind, up behind his plane. The second I judged I was in range, about three hundred feet where all six guns converged, I pulled the trigger. My plane shook with the recoil power of the six .50 calibers. Tracers, every third round, lined toward the plane and converged on the cockpit, sending pieces of the canopy exploding away from the plane. Parts of the fuselage around the cockpit ripped away. I was momentarily shocked by the destructive power of the bullets. The Hellcat was one damn powerful weapon.

The Japanese pilot banked hard left in a steep, tight turn while I watched our two planes closing in on each other, thinking, *Is he trying to ram me?* He flashed past my left wingtip, going straight down. I never saw him again. I believe he was mortally wounded and had made one final effort to take me with him. We continued flying in our dominant high position, ready to pick off other unsuspecting planes.

Mac banked left, the four of us scanning the sky, looking for another enemy. We had been over the target running at full throttle long enough to consume the 150 gallons in our belly tanks, which we had dropped earlier—our main tanks were rapidly draining. It was time to leave. We descended, threading our way through the hills and low rain clouds, heading back to the carrier.

Once over the sea, we reduced the pitch of our propellers to conserve fuel. By sliding behind Brooks, I could see the ghost image of his prop and altered the pitch of my propeller so that it matched his three-bladed image. My engine was then in sync with his, consuming fuel at the same relative rate.

On the way back, one of our guys, Joe Kopman, radioed his fuel amount to Johnny Johnson, concerned about having enough to get back to the ship. I checked mine and had more than he did, and we were ahead of him. I heard Joe's final call to Johnny when his engine quit. We watched him make a water landing, but he never got out of the plane. When we landed on the carrier, I only had 30 gallons left.

Years later, friends asked what it felt like to kill someone, what kind of emotions went through my brain when the .50-caliber bullets from my guns blasted into a Japanese plane, at times seeing the enemy pilot as I held my finger down on the trigger. Destroying the Tony was done without passion. It was done with trained precision.

Back aboard the ship after the flight, the excitement was really one of triumph. In reality, it was one plane against another, each pilot knowing only one of us would come back alive. One couldn't afford emotion or a moment of hesitation because the least amount of sentiment would result in death.

My personal thoughts about killing others these many years after the war—well, that's another very private story that only I discuss with myself.

Codine

- 57 -

Codeine is a nice drug.
It lets sleep in and delays fear.
With the burden of fear, there is no sleep.
Death is the fear and my subconscious companion.
In the brightness of daylight, fear lurks in the shadows of my mind,
waiting, a nocturnal being,
aloof and beyond suppression.

I checked in with Doc Moy. Between the heat of the bunk room and my anxiety, I was unable to sleep. I would stay in the air-conditioned ready room until around midnight and then went to the bunk room and tried to sleep a few hours.

I knew the effect lack of sleep could cause, and running mostly on adrenaline was much too dangerous. My life and the lives of my copilots depended on quick, sound, and alert judgment. Doc understood the situation well. He gave me a codeine pill every evening, which calmed me down, and I was able to sleep.

Once aboard a ship for a length of time, you notice that ships smell electric. It's part of a ship's delicacy. You can smell the electric hum just as you can hear it. It is a strong sound, the sound of a vessel driving on its compass course, bow smashing through the night, lifting an artistic phosphorescent spray of ocean amoebae—dazzling and electrifying. The ship drives on, riding the Pacific swells in a gentle, rolling twenty-seven-thousand-ton waltz with over three thousand men as her captive guests.

The electric noise worked itself into my ear's silence as I lay awake on my mat and sprung, one among forty-one other breathing, sweating, frightened bodies, all suspended in this electric vacuum. The embrace of codeine was over, spent like another night's brief love affair. The sweat of the three-tiered bodies in the junior officer's bunk room emitted a cloak of heat and stench that suffocated.

The overhead above the bunk room was laced with handmade cardboard tubing designed to channel relief, hooked up with the ship's inadequate pressurized air ducts, providing blithe notions of fresh air. Ducts diverted and bifurcated, meant to breathe cool hopes on hot, sweat-drenched bodies all in some crazy fake quilt pattern. A shrine of tunnels and cardboard hoses—poured warm air from three nozzles onto my forehead, navel, and penis.

My mat was an island of security and hope. I longed to sink from the heaviness of fear into sleep, but the smell and the electric hum just seemed to get louder. Footsteps sounded on the deck above, muffled by armor-plated steel. There was a distant hissing sound as the mighty bow of the ship forced the sea aside. Toothbrushes, razors, and combs made their irritating scraping sounds as they slid from side to side in the metal cabinets above the shell sinks, waltzing to the ship's sway, their rhythm metronomic.

There was an odd nonsilence. I lay awake and read my black-faced watch—0230. I awoke and started to think of the chain of events that would begin in an hour in the middle of the Pacific Ocean. Priceless sleep—sleep to erase all thought, sleep to put off coming events that can only be imagined, sleep, the safe cradle, only sleep.

The yeoman started down the ladders in the carrier's island at 0320, heading forward to awaken the officers scheduled for the predawn takeoff. He crossed the hangar deck, passing weary-eyed mechanics to check on the fighters. Up the ladder to the forecastle deck, he tested his red-hooded flashlight.

I was in the middle of a stressful dream. In my dream, I was enrolled in the first semester of college. Things seemed OK, but then I realized that it was not the first semester—it was midterm, and I hadn't attended my class in history. Suddenly, I was taking the final exams, and I hadn't attended history or English classes in months. I didn't even know what history we were on—European or American? What century were we in? *Good god! I 'm going to fail. What can I do?* I was rolling; I was shaking. I can't get the fear of failure out of my head.

The sailor with the red-hooded flashlight was pumping my shoulder. "Sir, it's 0330."

I awoke to the now and the immediate future.

187

The Battle Of Leyte Gulf

- 58 -

In October 1944, the US Navy landed four Sixth Army divisions ashore on Leyte. Later in the day, Gen. Douglas A. MacArthur gave his "I have returned" radio message to the Philippine people. He had previously departed the Philippines in March 1942 saying, "I will return." For the Japanese, should Leyte be lost, the rest of the Philippines would soon follow, so they prepared an offensive by sending five strong naval forces to drive off the American fleet. In the following days, this response would lead to World War II's biggest and most complex sea battle, the multipronged Battle of Leyte Gulf.

We had come south from Okinawa. No American force had been that close to Japan since Doolittle's famous raid on the Japanese islands. Anticipating the possibility of pilots being shot down and confronting the Chinese people who may have been fearful of Americans due to propaganda, we were issued little 3" × 4" cards, which had a blue and red Taiwan flag on the top left corner and the Stars and Stripes on the top right corner. Down the center of the card, between the flags, were Chinese characters that said, "I'm best friend with Chinese." They were not the enemy, but it never hurt to play all the odds.

As we came south, we hit Aparri and Formosa in Taiwan, skipping the Pescadores, which were removed from the original strike plan.

The strategic hits on these islands south of Japan were calculated to neutralize them. The plan was for the Philippines to be used as both the US air and ground staging area for the conquest of Japan.

We continued to lose pilots. Dick Bridge, a good friend and squadron mate from Detroit, was struck by enemy fire and was reported hit while strafing a radio station on Formosa.

Gen. Douglas MacArthur—commander of all army, navy, and marine forces—set October 20, 1944, as W-Day so as not to be confused with D-Day, the June Allied landings in France. MacArthur's command ship was the heavy cruiser *Nashville*. The Third Fleet was providing cover for 430 transports, which were steaming north with 174,000 men of the Sixtieth Army with the fire support of Admiral Kinkaid's Seventh Fleet.

After our forces hit the Leyte beach, the Japanese responded with the Sho-Go plan—a last attempt of the Japanese Imperial Navy, hoping a huge defense would tire the already weary US forces and come to a compromise that would end the war. It was a reactionary plan. The Japanese plan was for their First Attack Force to move from the north across the Sibuyan Sea and through the strait. The Japanese Second Attack Force and Force C would move from the south across the Mindanao Sea through the Surigao Strait. This action precipitated the most decisive air-sea battle of World War II—the Battle of Leyte Gulf.

On October 23, American submarines of the Seventh Fleet intercepted the first attack group as they moved into position southwest of Leyte and sank two heavy Japanese cruisers west of Palawan, which ignited the battle. A series of virtually continuous surface and air confrontations followed, with the heaviest in the Sibuyan Sea. The Third Fleet, under Admiral Halsey, was lured by the Japanese into a pointless pursuit of a group of stripped-down aircraft carriers. Halsey grabbed the bait, gut hooked, and roared after the decoy, leaving the rest of the American fleet vulnerable. He played a bad hand of poker that came to be known as Bull's Run.

Aboard ship, in the thick of the battle, knowledge at our level was limited to our orders and carrying out our missions. The scuttlebutt was that we were to destroy some of the most important ships in the

Japanese Navy. We were instruments of war about to be deployed against a huge enemy force while playing out our role in the master plan. We could only hope and trust Halsey had the winning plan against the Japanese admiral Kurita. We were just as pebbles on a beach.

On October 24, the three major engagements of the battle were fought almost simultaneously. Battleships and cruisers of the Seventh Fleet destroyed Japan's C Force and forced their Second Attack Force to withdraw while the enemies First Attack Force sailed through the unguarded San Bernardino Strait and heavily damaged carriers off Samar. Unexpectedly, they withdrew instead of attacking the landing operation off Leyte.

In the north off Cape Engaño, part of the Third Fleet sank the Japanese decoy carriers while our group moved south, pursuing and attacking Japan's First Attack Force. During the battle, air group commanders and skippers from different carriers were assigned periods during which they would direct attacks on the Japanese fleet, which was now desperately trying to retreat. It was known at this point in the war that the Japanese pilots were understaffed, overworked, and mainly undertrained.

Brooks, Smith, and I were assigned to fly with Commander Kibbe, a target coordinator. The flight was almost six hours long, most of it spent circling the stricken enemy ships. Kibbe was directing wave after wave of fighters, dive-bombers, and torpedo bombers from different carriers as they dived through intensive ack-ack, sending bombs, rockets, and .50-caliber machine-gun fire into the hulls of the surrounded enemy ships, which by now were in a circular formation, "circling the wagons," trying to mount their collective firepower against the attacking planes diving down at them out of the clear blue sky.

Kibbe, while directing aerial traffic and target selection, had us circle the spectacle in loose formation as his honor guard, keeping just high enough to remain out of range of the ship's guns. Circling this historic battle, we became a battle in the air within a battle on the sea. One of the Japanese destroyers was tracking us. The destroyer would cut across the circle of ships, rapidly moving to the opposite side at flank speed, white wake churning, following, and trying to get us within her sights. Seeing this, Kibbe would playfully have us nose down, losing a little altitude while bringing us almost within range of the ship's guns, tempting the Japanese AA, almost like waving a bird feather wand in front of a cat. Taking the bait, the destroyer would fire, and their shells exploded beneath our formation, not close enough to cause damage but near enough to be damn frustrating and demoralizing to the Japanese as we would swiftly pull up out of their range.

We were part of Halsey's Raiders. Major Japanese carriers and battleships had been sunk. Those were stunning moments, seeing Japan's once powerful lethal warships now as harmless huge sinking hulks.

Leyte was the largest naval battle of WWII and most likely the largest naval battle in history. It was also the death knell for the Japanese effort.

Brooksie

- 59 -

Admiral Davison's air groups were nearing exhaustion. The hours, days, and months of intense combat stress were grinding down everyone's resolve. New reserve pilots, strangers to our Fighting Thirteen, were being sent to the ship, called up to fill our depleted ranks. Senior pilots were flying less and less. McGraw, who served his first tour on the *Enterprise*, said that his earlier tour couldn't compare with the amount of intense flying hours and fighting we had done.

So it was that Lieutenant Junior Grade Brooks was leading eight planes on a late afternoon fighter sweep on the Dulag beaches. The flight was composed of Lt. (j.g.) Bill Parsons, Ensign Jim O'Donnell, Ensign Bill Dorie, Ensign Jim Pope, Ensign Bill Nygren, Ensign McQuady, and Ensign Mewborn. Their mission was to strafe enemy forces and conduct a coordinated close attack to pave the way for the advance of ground troops. Except for McQuady and Mewborn, they were an experienced but now tired group.

I can still visualize Brooks wearing standard navy flight gear—sweat-stained tan flight coveralls, a navy-issue black-faced wristwatch that glowed in the dark like my dad's Big Ben alarm clock, and his parachute harness with a backpack. He wore his ankle-length Marine Corps jungle boots, a cloth helmet with goggles snapped in place, and radio earphones encased in the helmet's ear pockets, phone jack swinging loose, with a green rubber oxygen mask snapped to the left side of his helmet, a Mae West, and his .38-caliber revolver. His hands were gloved in light pigskin, which were mandatory for all navy pilots. The gloves weren't a matter of style; they were a matter of survival. A pilot bailing out of a burning plane with burned hands would have great difficulty pulling the rip cord of their parachutes.

All VF-13 pilots wore red cowboy bandannas tied around their neck, slung with a certain cocky air of defiance. The squadron had adopted the nickname "cowboys" before we left the States when Deacon Parsons, one of our more persuasive members, bartered a few tidbits to acquire enough of these neckerchiefs to outfit the group. He also bartered for our nonregulation white helmets. Sartorial elegance aside, the bandannas were useful as emergency tourniquets. The fighters wore those red banners as a sign of camaraderie and squadron strength with a little ego and swagger thrown in. Under his arm, Brooks carried a Mark III plotting board pencil marked with the carrier's launch position, recovery position, and his course to the target and back.

The squawk box ordered, "Fighter pilots, man your planes!"

The ten assigned pilots rose from our squadron ready room seats and headed out the rear hatch through the passageway to the port-side catwalk and up the ladder to the flight deck. As he left the ready room, Brooksie stopped, looked over at me, and said, "Goldbrick." It was just one word with a sarcastic smirk and a backhanded wave, and on he went. He called me Goldbrick for slacking because I wasn't flying with him that afternoon. Doc Moy had lanced a carbuncle on my back and grounded me until it healed—an irritation from months of chafing by the survival pack on the parachute harness.

Lt. (j.g.) Robert Brooks and I had flown together since 1943. I was his wingman; he was my section leader. This would be the last time I saw Brooksie.

Brooks was from Windsor, Connecticut, tough, short, bombastic, irascible, and outspoken. A seasoned airman, he was on his second combat tour, having been on the *Hornet* during an earlier tour of duty.

I grew to know the real Brooks, who was a very private person, very sensitive—a young man with strong church roots he never revealed.

According to Bill Dorie, when they arrived on tactical combat air patrol (TCAP) over the Leyte shore, they were jumped by Tonys and Zeros. At one point in the scrambling dogfight, Dorie ran out of gas in his auxiliary tank and was able to switch tanks, and then the engine caught, and he shot down a Tony. The dogfight continued, and when it was over, Brooks, Parsons, Pope, Dorie, and the others joined up in the descending darkness. With deteriorating weather quickly setting in, they landed in a field that was a rough fighter strip in the jungle about a mile from the coast. Dodging numerous shell holes in the dirt strip, all landed except Brooks, who was lagging behind alone.

Dorie said, "We were no sooner on the ground than a Zero came tearing up the runway about twenty feet in the air, going like a bat out of hell. I don't remember him firing his guns. I suspect it was more an act of defiance. He pulled up and disappeared."

Now darker and darker by the minute, Brooks still in the air, Parsons and Dorie got back up on one of the Hellcat's wings, turned on the radio, and listened to the tower contacting Brooks, giving him landing clearance. "He started his approach," Dorie remembered. "And every gun in the area let loose, thinking it was that damn Zero again. Brooksie tried twice, but then I distinctly remember him saying, 'To hell with this. I'm going out over the bay and bail out.' We assumed he'd be picked up routinely and returned to the ship eventually."

Nothing is certain about Brooks's fate. Perhaps he died attempting a water landing during the bedlam of that night. He might have also been mistaken for a Japanese plane as he attempted to land or bail out in the darkness, shot down by friendly fire from one or many of the hundreds of boats in the American invasion fleet anchored off the shores of Leyte. He was officially listed as missing in action.

I've always thought Brooks felt superstitious because I wasn't flying on his wing that afternoon. How did I feel about his loss? It's hard to put into words. While what seemed like a long time ago, we gathered after the loss of Kelly, where I could hardly contain my emotions in the ready room, this was different. It wasn't that I was hardened to all the deaths and losses I had seen by now. It was just an emotion I learned to tuck away deep down inside and not let come to the surface. I knew, for my own sake, I had to put Brooks out of my mind but never out of my heart.

Divine Wind

- 60 -

V. Adm. Takijiro Onishi, the commander of Japan's First Air Fleet ordered to take command of the air fleet's impending battle, was "horrified" after the Imperial Japanese Navy lost hundreds of their pilots and aircraft. There was not nearly enough airpower to fulfill his plans of attack or defense. What we didn't expect and were about to encounter was what the Japanese named *kamikaze* or "divine wind" for the sudden typhoon that had saved Japan from a Mongol invasion fleet during the thirteenth century.

Japan's hold on the Philippines was weakening day by day. The American fleets were now in command. Onishi stated, "There is only one way of assuring that our meager strength will be effective to a maximum degree. That is to organize suicide attack units composed of A6M Zero fighters armed with 250-kilogram bombs, with each plane to crash-dive into an enemy carrier."

Kamikazes were volunteers, many of them young university students, motivated by loyalty to country and reverence for the emperor. Their training was hasty for a task that required less expertise than resolve. This effort was instilled with the repetitive slogans that their "nobility of spirit" would be enough to save Japan. "Wrapped in religious scarves," young pilots vowed to use their flying skill, often quite minimal, to plunge their planes heavily loaded with bombs and extra gasoline into the ships of the American fleet. This piloted missile was given the nickname "Baka" by the Allies from the Japanese word for "fool." The pilot had no means of getting out once the missile was fastened to the aircraft that would launch it.

Dropping usually from an altitude of over twenty-five thousand feet and more than fifty miles from its target, the missile would glide to about three miles from its target before the pilot turned on its three rocket engines, accelerating the craft to more than six hundred miles per hour in its final dive. The explosive charge built into the nose weighed more than a ton.

This suicide phenomenon managed to sink 34 Allied war vessels and damage 368 others, inflicting 9,700 casualties at the cost of about 4,000 young Japanese kamikaze pilots' lives. The effort was not a success. Unlike the divine wind that saved Japan from the Mongol invasion, these daring, very young, and mostly inexperienced kamikazes failed to turn back the American onslaught. After the August 1945 surrender of Japan, Admiral Onishi followed in the path of his dedicated yet doomed pilots by committing suicide in his quarters.

Battle Stations

- 61 -

The *Franklin*, which had maneuvered to within fifty miles of the Japanese mainland, closer than any other US carrier during the war, launched a fighter sweep against Honshu and later a strike against shipping in Kobe Harbor. The *Franklin* crew had been called to battle stations twelve times within just six hours that night. Battle stations sounded, sending all pilots to their ready rooms; the first six or ten fighter pilots to arrive were assigned to the emergency flight, the most senior officer serving as flight leader. Whatever the number of planes flying, there were always two pilots, the fifth and sixth or the ninth and tenth to arrive, assigned as standby pilots in their planes on deck, engines running, ready to fill in if one of the aircraft was given a "down," unable to fly because of some engine or mechanical problem. This ensured the flight complement was always full.

The call to battle found the first fourteen of us in the ready room assigned to provide fighter protection for supply ships under Japanese air attack 240 miles away. We hurried to our planes. I was the thirteenth fighter, number one standby. From my cockpit, I saw Cleboski pull to the port-side elevator, downed for mechanical reasons. I was brought forward, taking his place to wait for my turn to take off. I was the last in the air, and as soon as I flew off the deck, it was announced in urgent tones not to rendezvous ahead of the ship. "Depart the area immediately. Rendezvous en route."

I joined up with the other planes heading for the ships under attack. I noticed one of the pilots in the flight gestured back toward the fleet. I turned and saw a giant column of gray-black smoke rising straight up from a carrier. *Not our carrier,* I thought, *not the* Franklin. *Totally impossible.* Without looking back, we went forward on a very lean mixture, increased manifold pressure, and low RPMs, props ticking over in a relatively high pitch, making every effort to conserve fuel. We had a long way to go and a long way back.

We arrived over the supply ships to find other fighters from another air group already there and no sign of the enemy. With props in normal pitch, we circled the ships for a few minutes and then checked out, heading back to home base using ZBX—our radio navigation homing device, which sent out Morse code letters in fifteen-degree segments to hone in on. Now preparing for landing, we were stunned, realizing the billowing smoke we saw was indeed coming from the *Franklin*—she had been hit. We divided up and landed on two different carriers, where we learned our home of steel was very badly damaged.

We were transported back to the *Franklin* from the carriers via a boatswain's chair—a canvas sling with lines strung together, first from the *San Jacinto* to the *Gridley,* a destroyer, and then from the destroyer up to Big Ben. Being hauled between two ships while sitting in a canvas seat dangling from ropes, the ships steering parallel courses, sailors pulling the lines that hauled me from one ship to the other, lines dipping down as the ships rolled with the sea, the ocean coming up to meet my feet clad in my trusty oxfords, I thought, *There isn't much more left to see.* I was wrong. What I would see would remain with me forever.

Kamikaze Damage

- 62 -

Once back aboard the *Franklin*, I saw the impact of the kamikaze's damage. The hole in the deck measured forty feet across, exactly where my plane had been parked as number one standby, the thirteenth plane. The explosion went down four decks, killing fifty-four men with three not expected to live and wounding many others. The deck was warped by the force of the explosion. Steel plates were buckled and torn; hatches and bulkheads crumpled like tin foil. The number three elevator was destroyed. The ship's interior was covered with a thick film of black soot that carried the stench of the fire. The water in our ready room was several inches deep. Men had been manning pumps all night to clear water from flooded spaces.

Adm. Bull Halsey came aboard for a brief period to inspect the damage. I was on the flight deck when he and his aides appeared from within the ship's island. All hands on the flight deck froze to attention. He silently and gravely viewed the damage. Then he turned to us and gave the *Franklin*'s men and officers a quick and proud salute, saying, "Well done."

When order was restored after the kamikaze attack, the painful task of burials at sea took place. I can still see the flag-draped bodies on planks lined up at the forward port side of the flight deck, flags held in place by the pallbearers, not to be released until the bodies were sent over the side of the ship to their permanent resting place at sea. All men who were not on watch assembled in formation on the flight deck while the chaplains read the final funeral services. Then taps played while the assembly stood at attention, and the ship slowed almost to a halt. After a gun salute, each body—sewn in heavy canvas and weighted—was slid one by one into the calm Pacific Ocean, which would become their final resting place.

All hands on the Big Ben—the ship's company, the marine contingent, and air group personnel—led heroic lives because of their patriotic commitment and their belief in our country. My self-deprecating tendency dilutes the word *hero*, not wanting to label falsely nor praise unwisely. But for me, the dead were the only true heroes. They had made the ultimate sacrifice—their lives.

The crew cleaning up battle damage
(Courtesy of Bernard Groenewold)

Regroup

- 63 -

Admiral Davison now transferred his flag to the *Enterprise* while Capt. Leslie E. Gehres assumed command of Big Ben, relieving Captain Shoemaker. We retired to the atoll Ulithi for safety, repairs, and reassessment. So far, the divine wind succeeded in sinking forty ships and damaged hundreds more during these last stages of the war.

The rumors aboard were flying like shrapnel—the air group was going to regroup at Manus Island, the ship was going to Hawaii to be repaired, and we would get replacement pilots and be sent back out again on a different carrier. The prevailing scuttlebutt, the one we wanted to believe, was that we would stay with the *Franklin* no matter where she went. Most of the speculation carried with it the prospect that we would continue to be engaged in combat for an undecided number of additional months, not a happy thought. While none of us would readily admit it, we really were drained both emotionally and physically.

The hours and hours of back-to-back combat, the seemingly endless air patrols, the sleep deprivation layered by nerves, and the constant noise of takeoffs, catapult shots, and landings aboard all made for a worn-out group. We had faced our fear quotient every day and every night. As resilient as we had been thus far and still felt we were, admittedly to a lesser degree after the divine wind blew through our decks, we sensed the possibility of a much-needed respite, a chance that we might be spared for at least a restoration leave.

Cap Coleman's recommendation was that we be returned to the States. Now a full commander, the skipper had received new orders. He was transferred to Air Group Eighteen, where he would be commander of the air group (CAG) on the *Intrepid*.

After the squadron's formal farewell to the skipper in the ready room, those of us in the first and second divisions went down to the gangway on the hangar deck to pipe him over the side and say goodbye to the man who had skillfully led us through months of battle. There was no emotion, yet each handshake was an unspoken thank-you along with a wish for good luck—his as well as ours.

After days of waiting, the decision was announced. We were to stay with the ship, which departed Ulithi and headed for Guam for repairs and supplies. The possibility existed that the ship could be repaired in Hawaii.

At 0630 on November 7, 1944, my twenty-third birthday, I stood next to the cordoned-off section of the deck. As a junior aviator, I was assigned to the 0400 to 0800 security watch now that we were unable to fly. In the early light, I watched as scores of B-29s of the newly formed Twentieth Air Force rose into the sky, loaded with bombs, heading for Japan. So far, the Marianas strategy was successful. The grand plan was working.

Decompression

- 64 -

It turned out that Big Ben couldn't be repaired in Hawaii, where we laid over for a few days. We headed stateside, course set for the navy yard at Bremerton, Washington, where the ship would undergo major reconstructive surgery. The trip to the West Coast seemed much longer than our five-day sprint to Hawaii seven days ago.

Leaving the Pacific, moving through Puget Sound to the navy yard, was slow going—our minds raced ahead. We were more than eager to disembark from our home of steel. The air group had temporary orders to NAS Seattle, where we would decompress before going on a much needed and more than welcome thirty-six-day leave.

Air Group Thirteen had destroyed or damaged at least 338 enemy planes, sunk 60 merchant ships, damaged 66 merchantmen, sunk 15 warships, and flown 3,971 combat sorties against the enemy. *Decompression* is my word for the seven days we spent at NAS Seattle before being released for our rest and recuperation leave. The press held meetings to interview those with dramatic experiences and heroic stories to report to the public from firsthand experience. We were checked out by navy MDs, and our teeth, after long overdue checkups, were filled, cleaned, or pulled by navy dentists. We were becoming physically and mentally fit to return home or wherever we wanted to go for the next thirty-six days. I believe the navy didn't want to release us directly from combat into civilian life perhaps for fear that we were still a little crazed and battle worn and needed a grace period to smooth back into a social life in the States.

Rehabilitation wasn't an operative word then, but that was what was happening. You never knew where therapy was going to come from or what form it might take. There was only so much the navy could do to assist us from constant high alert to smooth and slow.

One evening Will Gove, Bill Bowman, A. J. Pope, and I went into Seattle with no plan in mind, just happy as hell to be stateside. We meandered along one of the downtown sidewalks, four fighter pilots without a dawn sweep in the horizon. As we crossed a street, four very pretty young ladies passed. One said to the other three, "Do you think they might like to dance?" Four smiling fighter pilots did an instant smart military about-face. The young women were students at the University of Washington, and their big prom just happened to be that night. Would we like to go?

Since "dancing" was my middle name, I promptly and politely replied, "We'd be delighted."

We agreed to meet the ladies in about half an hour in the lobby of the hotel where the dance was taking place; they jumped in a cab, off to get into their formals. Smiling and looking lovely, they arrived with the tickets, and we danced the night away, back in civilization with lovely girls in our arms. I felt surprised hearing a lot of popular songs that were completely new to me, asking my date the names of the songs as though I had just returned from Mars. What a difference a year makes. Rehabilitation couldn't have been sweeter than that December 1944 evening in Seattle.

I'll Be Home For Christmas

- 65 -

With the exception of Christmas 1942, when I was a cadet in preflight at the University of Iowa, the confluence of the air group's schedule and Christmas allowed me to be home for the holiday every year—'43, '44, '45, and '46. For our small Christian family, this was a gift like no other.

My parents and I were fortunate that they were able to attend many of the major events before I went into battle. They had attended my graduation ceremony and commissioning in Texas. My mother came to Melbourne for a short visit during operational training, and when the USS *Franklin* was commissioned in Newport News, Virginia, my mother and father came down for the onboard ceremony and the squadron party afterward. In the spring of 1945, they visited me while we were training at Livermore, California, staying at a hotel in San Jose that Bill Dorie and I buzzed one day, hoping they would see us showing off—they didn't. All their travel was by train. As a supervisor at Kelsey-Hayes Wheel Company, my dad was fortunate to be able to take time away from his job.

Now in mid-December, I was leaving Seattle on my way home for a thirty-six-day R&R leave—with orders to report to NAS Oakland in San Francisco Bay on a specified date in January 1945. We would regroup there, with new pilots joining us "old" veterans. The air group had a distinguished record. We had developed polish and perfection during our first combat tour, which would be a challenge to maintain; but for now, forget all that. It was home for Christmas.

I caught a navy transport plane headed east, the durable Douglas DC-3, a twin-engine plane with a restricted range. The trip across the country would be made in a series of flights, their length determined by the plane's load, fuel capacity, rate of fuel consumption, and weather. Flying cross-country in midwinter meant probable nasty weather, and so delays were to be expected.

Approaching North Platte, Nebraska, our next fuel stop, we encountered such a solid overcast that the pilot and copilot had to make an instrument approach to the field. The plane was filled with officers, many of them navy and marine pilots, along with a few enlisted men, all battle veterans hooking a ride home for their holiday leave. In those days, an instrument landing approach was rudimentary at best, consisting of Morse code signals beamed from the active runway. Establishing his approach, the pilot began a specific rate of descent, maintaining course, waiting to break through the cloud layer and approach for a wheel landing.

I was sitting by a window on the port side, watching for a break in the clouds, hoping to see land. The pilot's cabin was visible to most of the passengers, which allowed us to watch them at work. We were combat-weary men heading home, now in a chancy circumstance, all of us fully aware that our lives were in the hands of the two navy pilots at the controls, flying the transport on instruments through the clouds, heading safely toward the ground. It was a strange feeling as we were veteran pilots now strapped in as passengers, each of us mentally flying the plane.

We broke through the overcast at about four hundred feet in perfect alignment with the runway and touched down, the two tires chirping as they met the concrete, the plane slowing, the tail lowering until the third wheel, the tail wheel, hit the runway. The landing completed, we taxied toward the small airport building. We applauded the pilot and copilot. "Well done" and "congratulations" came from a bunch of war pilots.

Faced with more delays and an uncertain weather forecast, I decided to complete the trip to Detroit by train. It felt good to be home, surrounded by my parents' love, plus finally a perfect night's quiet sleep in my own bed at 9333 Monica Ave. in Detroit, the automotive capital of the world. The winter was starkly cold and blustery with hardly any snow, just freezing temperatures. The front door of our house opened directly into the living room, which when left open would allow a cold blast into the room. Perhaps I felt the cold more, having become accustomed to the balmy Pacific heat. My favorite spot in the house was in front of the living room hot air register, heat blowing up from the coal furnace in the basement. My aunt Dolly, uncle Russ, and cousin David came down from Grand Rapids to join the Christmas celebration.

Dad and Uncle Russ had endless questions—where I'd been, what engagements I'd been in, which invasions, all that had happened during the past seven months since the ship left Hawaii, headed for combat. They got out their newspaper clippings along with maps of the Pacific and all the notes they had made while playing their game of "where is he?", trying to determine if they were right in tracking where the task force was. War information had been very limited, severely censored, and very vague, making it almost impossible for them to have a clear idea of the ship's destinations. At times, they were shocked at how wrong they had been. Their estimates of ship movement and battles, their guesses about the location of the *Franklin*, seemed to stun them. When they discovered some of their guesses were correct, they felt as victorious as though they had won first prize in a game contest.

They did pretty well, considering they weren't getting enough solid information for reasonable conjecture. Nor did they know the speed the task force was capable of, which was part of the master plan to confuse the Japanese into thinking that we had more aircraft carriers than we did. The navy's strategy was to strike for two or three days and then withdraw and race to another area. The navy tactic fooled the Japanese, and along with the strict censorship, they fooled my dad and my uncle Russ as well.

Winding Down At Home

- 66 -

After a few days of "feeling at home," I didn't need much rest or recuperation. I needed some fun and female companionship. Marge Shobe, my high school girlfriend, had kept a flow of letters coming to me while I was at sea, numbering them so I knew their sequence, even perfuming many of them. We renewed our romance and began to see a lot of each other again while I was home. Most of the dates we went on were to a small nightclub in Downtown Detroit that had a dance floor and comedy acts. They also held impromptu dance routines for couples with a prize, usually a free drink or fancy dessert, which we were pretty good at; and much to Marge's thrill, we won a few times. We both loved the double-feature Saturday night movies, starting with a newsreel, of course.

My mother didn't want me to get serious with Marge for fear I would repeat the same situation I had encountered with Mary once I would leave. I also dated Kay MacKenzie a couple of times, picking up where we had left off on the dating scene before Mary. Unbeknownst to me, during my holiday leave, Mary Knight's picture appeared in the *Detroit News* announcing her engagement. When the war was over, my mother told me Dad hid the paper and burned it in the furnace so that I wouldn't see it. I smile as I think about his tenderness—my father sharing my disappointment, knowing how hard I had been hurt, trying in his own way to protect his son.

Before we went home on leave, some of us had decided to call on the parents, wives, or family who resided near us and had a loved one who had been killed or was missing in action. We divided up names, and it turned out two of Fighting Thirteen's pilots who were killed and one torpedo pilot who was declared missing in action were from Detroit. I volunteered to make those calls.

The first phone call I made was to Joe Kopman's father, identifying myself as a squadron mate of his son. Mr. Kopman, without any hesitation, asked me what had happened to Joe. I told him that, after completing an extralong mission, Joe had run out of gas on the way back to the carrier—he made what appeared to be an excellent water landing, but no one saw him get out of the plane. Mr. Kopman was silent for several moments, and then he began hollering at me. "No! That's not true! That couldn't have happened. Why wouldn't he just have gotten out of the plane? That simply can't be true."

I tried to calm him and tell him that, at times, a swift water landing could leave a pilot stunned or disoriented or even unconscious, but Mr. Kopman lost control and raved on for a couple of minutes. I decided the best thing to do was to just listen to his outpouring of grief, and once he was quiet, I told him I was so sorry for his loss. Consumed by his anger, rage, and denial, he just wasn't listening. He was overcome with grief. I told him again that I was sorry for his loss and said goodbye. I was numbed by this sorrowful experience, and it made me stop and think about my parents and how heartbroken they would have been to receive such a call.

Not deterred, I made my second call to Mr. and Mrs. Bridge, Dick's parents. I told them that I was a friend of their son and home on leave. They were most cordial and invited me to visit them in Grosse Pointe, which I did several days later. They had tea and some refreshments prepared, and we sat and spoke about their son. Trying to cheer them, if that was possible, I told them some of the ship's more upbeat activities while they reminisced about his time at Oberlin College in Ohio. They managed to joke how Dick's wife, also a navy officer, outranked him, having received her commission earlier than he received his. I told them that Dick said his wife always chuckled at the way his shoes curled up at the toes. His dad told me Dick held the Grosse Pointe High School record in track for the school's fastest time in the 440-yard dash—so proud of his son's achievement.

Their hearts must have been breaking as I sat there with them while talking about Dick in their living room. They were truly as brave as Dick was. I visited with them a few more times, serving, I believe, as some kind of conduit to Dick, and I hoped I helped ease their pain just a little. Their other son, Dick's elder brother whose name I've forgotten, was a captain in the infantry in Europe. I learned later that he too was killed in action, leaving the Bridge family bereft of their two young sons—a heartbreaking high price to pay.

Before I left for NAS Oakland and the squadron, I learned that the third condolence call I was supposed to make to Bob Freleigh's family, the VT-13 torpedo pilot who was shot down off Leyte, would turn out to be one of utmost joy. Bob had survived his water landing, and through sheer will, he managed to reach shore, where he and his crew were rescued. Best of all, he was now on his way home. His parents only knew that he was listed as missing in action, so at least one call I had to make brought the greatest news they could ever have received. By coincidence, Bob returned home while I was still on leave, and we spoke on the phone. His first words were "Damn, it's good to hear your voice, Bob."

The thirty-six days sped by. I had fun. I was rested and ready for the next Air Group Thirteen adventure. My parents now had to ready themselves for yet another departure.

Part Six

The War Is Over

Second Tour

- 67 -

Our air group was scheduled to return to combat only after we trained new pilots, but the divine wind changed our future as it did everyone's on the *Franklin*. Though we didn't know it at the time, combat in action ended for us when the kamikaze blasted through the deck of our ship. Despite this temporary pause for us in combat, the war was far from won, and we still lived on the edge, preparing for our second tour of duty and what was to be the invasion of Japan as a plan to finally end the war.

The squadron reformed at the naval air station in Alameda, California, on January 1, 1945. The squadron was commissioned as a component of Air Group Thirteen and, during this period, operated under Commander Fleet Air Alameda as a unit of the air force Pacific Fleet. The squadron would still operate as a carrier-based fighter unit.

With Lt. Jaye M. Sullivan now in command as of January 17, 1945, and Will Gove, executive officer, the squadron reformed in Alameda, taking on new pilots. We were then transferred to Naval Auxiliary Air Station Fallon, Nevada, where we resumed the good old navy fighter training syllabus—practice, practice, practice. We were slightly rusty after our long R&R leave, needing brushup air time, a lot of work to elevate our proficiency level and bring us back up to speed so we could, in turn, set the navy standards for the incoming pilots.

Many ensigns such as us returning to VF-13 had received promotions to lieutenant junior grade. We were given an option of change, and some of our original group decided not to continue with the squadron and join other squadrons instead. My core group of friends—Bowman, Dorie, Higgins, and Pope—all stayed together now that we were JGs. That extra half-stripe on our sleeves and shoulder boards had been hard earned, and we wore it proudly. We were now considered veterans, providing teaching and leadership for the new pilots. Lt. (j.g.) Howard Lay was my division leader; I was his section leader. Our division included Carl Watkins, Paul Sample, and John Chatfield—all new boys.

Occasionally, award ceremonies took place. The squadron would assemble on the tennis courts at NAS Fallon wearing our blues—the navy's formal winter uniform—while the citations were read and medals presented. Each citation was accompanied by a typewritten statement and signed by the authorizing navy officer or the secretary of the navy. I had been awarded my first as an ensign. The format was standard:

> In the name of the President of the United States, the Commander, Second Carrier Task Force, United States Pacific Fleet, presents this AIR MEDAL to
>
> ENSIGN ROBERT VERNON HUNGERFORD
> UNITED STATES NAVAL RESERVE
> for service as set forth in the following
> CITATION
>
> "For distinguishing himself by meritorious acts while participating in thirteen aerial strikes against the enemy of the Nansei Shoto, Formosa, and Luzon area from 10 October to 29 October 1944.

While participating in a fighter sweep near Luzon on 17 October 1944 he encountered a group of enemy aircraft and in the ensuing action assisted in the destruction of two of the opposing planes.

His skill and courage were at all times in keeping with the highest traditions of the United States Naval Service."

John S. McCain
Vice Admiral, US Navy

When the war ended, the navy announced that if you had flown twenty-five combat hours, you were entitled to a Distinguished Flying Cross. In my opinion, this diminished the medal's value for those who had won it for outstanding valor and performance. But I wasn't the one making the rules.

On one occasion during an award ceremony, I was reminded of a time while aboard the *Franklin* in the thick of the Pacific battles. I received a letter from Reese MacDonald, my CPT friend who became an army officer. He was assigned as an instructor at a flight training base in Texas after receiving his wings. He had written to tell me had been awarded an Air Medal for flying a specific number of training hours without having an accident. He was very proud of that medal and rightfully so. However, I was furious, yet I understood the medal's motivational value for the army's training program. I was a naval aviator—I believed we had to qualify under extremely strenuous and high standards, but then Reese wasn't making the rules either, and he was proud of his Air Medal, justifiably so.

After I received my first Air Medal, I was awarded two Gold Stars in lieu of second and third Air Medals. Those citations were signed by the secretary of the navy, James Forrestal. While we were proud of our awards, they were simply medals or certificates. We held much greater pride in our ability to have survived the life-threatening direct, head-to-head battles, more than often due to comradeship and team effort, which when I think about it was our biggest accomplishment—way beyond any singular medal.

Will Gove received the Navy Cross, the navy's highest award, for sinking a Japanese cruiser when his bomb was successfully aimed straight down one of the ship's smokestacks. Nineteen other Distinguished Flying Crosses were awarded to VF-13 pilots, none of them more dramatic than A. J. Pope's feat of downing a Japanese Betty amid a torrent of antiaircraft fire from our own ships against the Betty, which was attempting a torpedo run on the fleet. This all occurred at the very same time AJ was trying to land safely aboard. Almost all of us received an Air Medal, sometimes several for our combat exploits—all tributes to the skill and bravery of our squadron's aviators. Cap Coleman was awarded the Silver Star and the Distinguished Flying Cross.

Old Is New Again

- 68 -

The element of change is always intriguing. Even though many of us had crossed paths in various air groups, the squadrons were independent of one another, and pilots seldom went outside their squadron's nucleus. Within Fighting Thirteen, groups of friends kept together, the married pilots living separate lives from the wild-ass bachelor segment.

A new entertaining diversion emerged at Fallon and Livermore—a game called cowboy billiards played on the recreation room pool table. Four players competed against one another; the winner was the first to score twenty-one points. It was a bastard combination of pool and billiards using the one, two, and three balls. After the break, it was necessary to score a billiard before you could sink a ball. A billiard counted for two points, and pocketing a ball gave the player the value of the ball; thus, it was possible to keep going, running up the score unless the player scratched, in which case the player lost his turn and had to make a billiard again to get back into the game. A hot player could, and did on occasion, run up twenty-one points in one turn. There were some very good "sticks" and no lack of competition (or inflated egos) between us fighters.

In the flying department, our division practiced hours of aerobatics in formation. With Howie Lay leading, Carl Watkins on his wing, me flying section leader with either Paul Sample or John Chatfield on my wing, we performed a loop. Up, over, inverted, Carl tucked into Howie, myself off Howie's left wing, my wingman in close on my left. High over the Nevada desert, down out of the loop we roared, perfecting control of our Hellcats in unusual altitudes. We weren't showing off; we were building confidence in the new guys and refreshing ourselves as a new division. These were flying aerobatics we had used and the new guys would later use with us in the air in real battles. For now, we were investing knowledge, skill, confidence, and trust in one another.

Every weekend the port and starboard wings of the squadron alternated liberty in Reno, about sixty miles away. A couple of guys had cars, which we would pile into for a two-day blast of drinking and partying. It was still a time of automobile gas rationing—getting to Reno and back sometimes required midnight requisition raids on the air group's supply of one-hundred-octane aircraft fuel. The starboard wing had Friday and Saturday off, and the port wing had Sunday and Monday—we alternated days the next weekend. We always wore our ribbons, our "fruit salad," which designated our medals in the hope we would meet some girls, thinking that perhaps the impressive color plumage on our chests would attract some females. Let's face it, we were male birds fluffing and preening as male birds do.

Most of the few women staying at our hangout, the El Cortez Hotel, were in Reno for one thing—a quickie divorce. We young male birds found ourselves among older and, for us, mostly unattractive, matronly women. We dubbed one "the Flower Pot" for the dizzy hats she wore. But attraction is all in the eye of the beholder, and it was said that one of our guys was the recipient of her favors. It was just a rumor, of course—gentlemen don't tell.

Occasionally, some single young women would wander into our lair, not by chance, I suspect, and life would suddenly brighten. On those occasions, we ate, danced, drank, and had some simple, good fun. Deep down, I think we all were looking for "a kiss to build a dream on," all of us knowing that we were gypsies with uncertain futures. It was a time of grabbing some momentary happiness while it was there.

On one of those Reno forays, I met a lovely young woman who actually lived in town. She was blond, petite, pretty, and vivacious. Could romance have found me? Our lives came together on weekends when she and her sister showed up at the hotel, and we found we were not just attracted but also enjoyed each other's company. We skied, we went to the clubs, and we danced, she very well, which gave her high marks in that department—we had fun.

One evening after dinner at the hotel, she invited me to come home with her as her sister was away for a few days. As we walked the few blocks to her house, she turned toward me and said, "We haven't even kissed." So we did, arms wrapped around each other in the cold winter night while standing on the sidewalk. I hadn't kissed a girl in months and found her desirable lips as inviting as her personality. In spite of the cold, we stopped and kissed several times during our walk. I was eager.

As we walked toward what was to become our romantic evening, she said as casually as saying *I shampooed my hair this morning*, "I'm married to an army officer, a bombardier." She continued that he had been stationed at Tonopah, the army's bomber training base southeast of Reno, and he was now overseas.

She smiled, saying, "I wish I had met you first." Her casualness almost froze me in my steps. Did I miss a wedding ring? I glanced at her hand, and no, there was none. Now big-time alarms went off in my brain while my Episcopalian altar boy upbringing suddenly surfaced like bait at the end of a fishing pole. I was offended, I felt duped, and our romance turned to stone on the spot. I admit, perhaps I was simply too much of a romantic. I was never good at one-night stands, especially not with a wife of a fellow military man now facing who knew what overseas.

I saw her home, and once inside, we sat on a couch in her living room, me semiparalyzed while her loving expression slowly went from expectancy to puzzlement and then to complete annoyance. I bid her a polite good-night and slowly trudged back in the cold to the El Cortez. I had harbored romantic notions of love. Most likely, I still carried the idea of finding someone who had captured my heart the way Mary did. OK, I admit it, I was naive.

Where we were successful was in the drinking department, favoring shots and beers. We favored the deadly depth charge at the hotel bar—a shot of whiskey lowered into a glass of beer on the bar. We never left hanging out at the El Cortez unless it was to go to Mount Rose for an afternoon on the slopes, followed by hot Tom and Jerries or rum hot toddies in the lodge. Late afternoon, we would drive down the mountain and race to the hotel to prolong the binge, have dinner, party, and dance before securing to leave for the weary long drive back to Fallon by midnight. We were young, our old cars never turned into pumpkins, and somehow we always made it back to base on time and in one piece.

Wing of Fighters, Fallon Nevada

The Franklin Close To Destroyed

- 69 -

Secure at our base in the States, retraining ourselves and training new pilots, enjoying weekend leaves, and away from the thick of battle, we received the shattering news about "our home of steel." On March 19, 1945, the USS *Franklin* was fifty miles off the coast of Japan, participating in air strikes against the island of Honshu by Task Force Fifty-Eight. On deck were thirty-one armed and fueled aircraft about to be launched while more armed and fueled aircraft were in the hangar deck below. Capt. Leslie E. Gehres, a tough ex-aviator, was in command of the ship. The deck held 36,000 gallons of gas and 30 tons of bombs and rockets—a floating inferno.

The weary crew had been called to battle stations twelve times within the past six hours, and Gehres downgraded the ship's alert status, allowing his men a brief rest to enjoy a meal or catch up on much-needed sleep. Unbeknownst to all, a single Japanese aircraft—a Yokosuka D4Y, "Judy," dive-bomber—silently stitched in and out of a thin layer of stratus clouds, blending in while following American planes returning to their carriers. Suddenly, the Judy—undetected and catching the *Franklin* crew unaware—swiftly pierced its cloud cover and dropped two 550-pound semiarmor piercing bombs before the ship's gunners could fire.

Scenes of indescribable horror swept the ship. Men were blown right off the flight deck into the sea. Heads bobbed for miles in the bitterly cold water. Some were instantly burned to cinders in the searing, white-hot flash of flame that swept across the hangar deck. Others were trapped in the compartments below and suffocated by smoke. Scores were either drowned or literally torn into pieces by the stored rockets and bombs onboard, which were now ignited and were exploding in every direction. A solid sheet of flame rose four hundred feet over the carrier.

The *Franklin* was soon dead in the water without radio communications and broiling in the heat from enveloping fires. Soon destroyers in the fleet came to the rescue and fell astern of the carrier to perform rescue operations, hosing water and, with their bows against the side of the carrier, helping remove men trapped by fire and the wounded. Despite the ship listing at thirteen degrees and in dire condition, Captain Gehres refused to scuttle the *Franklin* as there were still many men trapped alive below deck. Countless deeds of heroism and superb seamanship saved the carrier and about two-thirds of the ship's complement.

Lt. (j.g.) Donald A. Gray, one of two men to receive the Medal of Honor, was an engineer who knew the ship's layout in detail. Groping his way through hot, smoke-filled dark corridors, he found an escape route. He proceeded to calmly lead over 300 men through flames, flood, and smoke, making several trips back and forth until the last man had been saved.

Lt. Cmdr. Joseph T. O'Callahan—a poet, track star, writer, mathematics professor, Jesuit priest, and the *Franklin's* Catholic chaplain—was awarded the other Medal of Honor. Throughout the chaos and despite a leg wound, he raced, administering the last rites, comforting the wounded, organizing firefighting and rescue parties, and helping dispose of hot bombs and shells below deck while organizing a crew to wet down magazines threatening to explode. By one account, "He seemed to be everywhere, noticeable by the white cross painted on his helmet, doing everything he could to help save lives and our ship." His was the only Medal of Honor awarded to a chaplain during World War II.

Just when things seemed to be under control, radar picked up a bogey four miles out—another Judy. The bomb looked unreal, several times bigger than the plane that released it, but the bomb missed, splashing two hundred yards to starboard and detonated in the sea. With a few guns still operational, a motley crew made up of yeoman, laundrymen, and two balers from the ship's band along with a few others scrambled to man guns and splashed the Judy.

The heavy anchor was cut through, and a steel cable attached to the anchor chain enabled the *Pittsburgh* to slowly tow the damaged *Franklin* away from Japan at three knots. Captain Gehres now had time to call muster and take stock. His ship had 832 dead and almost 300 wounded. No ship in history had suffered such damage and losses yet still remained afloat.

Next came the garish, brutal task of burial detail as the dead now outnumbered the living left aboard the crippled ship. A member of the ship's band, whose duty it was to be a stretcher bearer, described his task as being more horrific than all the fire, fear, and explosions. Gathering the pitiful state of bodies either burned to a crisp or in scattered pieces was almost beyond endurance. The bodies or, in many cases, the body pieces were placed in weighted canvas bags and buried at sea with minimum ceremony other than prayers and the traditional gun salute. The burial task took several days to complete.

It took our squadron time to absorb all this. We had lived, celebrated, and worked with many of those onboard. While each of us dealt with sorrow in our own way, I had one thought. *There but for the grace of God go I.* Somehow someone was watching over me. The *Franklin* would become an epic of naval history warfare.

Preparing For The Invasion

- 70 -

The navy maintained a strict rule about wearing one's oxygen mask when flying at ten thousand feet and above. The amounts regulated according to altitude. The higher you climbed, the more oxygen was fed into your mask.

When we were cadets, we were put through oxygen/altitude tests so that we could experience the effects of loss of air in our brains and the impairment it caused. Groups of about twelve were seated in a low-pressure steel chamber. Starting at sea level, we were taken up higher and higher without masks while supervised by a seaman who wore a mask. Each cadet had a tablet on which to write his name over and over. As the altitude in the chamber climbed to ten thousand feet and above, it slowly became physically difficult to use the pencil, and our writing turned into unintelligible scrawls with frightening rapidity.

During my ascent, one cadet suddenly slumped over. Quick application of the cadet's mask by the seaman brought him back to consciousness. Masks were provided for each of us, and when oxygen deprivation had made its point, we strapped on our masks and slowly returned to the earth. In the Hellcats, oxygen flow could be manually set at 100 percent. There was nothing like pure oxygen to cure a hangover on a morning after some Reno escapade, even though we were flying field carrier landing practice at less than one hundred feet.

Flying over the bleak plains, plateaus, and mountain ridges of Nevada, we prepared for what we thought would soon be our destiny, covering the Japanese landscape during the possible invasion. The syllabus was designed to cover all the following:

- Familiarization
- Section tactics
- Division tactics
- Fixed gunnery
- Strafing
- Rocket firing
- Defensive tactics
- Offensive tactics
- Dive-bombing
- Glide-bombing
- Low-level bombing
- Instrument flights
- Night flying

In spite of being temporarily removed from combat at sea and safely in the States, we weren't excused from danger. Two of our new guys, Nikolay Liszak and Paul Spendley, both died in training accidents. There were also eight less serious accidents, and four aircraft were recommended to be struck.

At the finish of the syllabus at Fallon, the squadron packed its gear; and in April 1945, all units were moved to Livermore, California—my old training E base from years ago, now an operational field for fleet aircraft. We left ahead of the dive-bombers and torpedoes for our new assignment. After stowing our flight bags in the small luggage bay of the fighters, we took off, rendezvousing with Gove, who was leading the flight.

Will decided our stay should always be remembered by the Fallon Air Station, so he called for all thirty-six fighters to buzz the field.

Accepting Will's invitation to say goodbye to the base, Fighting Thirteen did its part, swooping down division after division, raking the field, free spirits leaving with a mighty roar. All planes sped down the runway just feet above the concrete. I eased down over parked TBFs as close as I dared and then bent left to zoom down a taxiway just for the fun of it. What the hell, there was no one in harm's way. I pulled up, gaining altitude, and all of us regrouped by divisions.

I guess it was our last retraining hurrah. Goodbye, Reno. Goodbye, Fallon. Fighting Thirteen was confident, trained, ready, and moving toward what we were sure was finally the end of the war.

California, Back Again

- 71 -

Leaving Reno, Will's navigation was right on target. We went straight to Naval Air Station Livermore, California, after a short and scenic side tour of beautiful Lake Tahoe, viewed from high altitude. Over Livermore, it felt strange to look down on the familiar rectangular field once again, my old E base. Now under very different circumstances, I was circling it in a fighter Hellcat while flooded with memories of our training days of circling this same field in a Stearman trainer.

The air group's young bucks took up residence in the BOQ across the street from the southeast corner of the field. We had commodious accommodations on the ground floor with a bar in the recreation room along with my upbeat salvation, a piano on the second floor. Bill Dorie and I roomed together just as we had at Fallon.

Trivia now, but at the time, little things were memorable, and one of the important things during those tension release moments were the liberal portions of Scotch at twenty-five cents a shot. On numerous weekends, a navy busload of Stanford University coeds arrived from Palo Alto for Saturday evening dances. These lovely young women were suddenly faced with a phalanx of fighter pilots almost like wolves, grinning near the entrance to the room, as they formed a cluster of safety, entering our den. Startled, almost fawnlike, the thirty or so women instinctively swerved to an immediate refuge—the ladies' room, of course. They all couldn't occupy such a small space at the same time, so we, convinced that we were charming and suave, moved in—gentlemen attired in smart military uniforms seeking a word or two while welcoming our guests.

I connected with a brunette, who when seated at the bar ordered her drink of choice, a Scotch, neat, in a pony glass. While we sat at the bar, becoming acquainted, she sipped her drink(s). I, being Mr. Bon Vivant, matched her drink for drink. While she remained as coherent as the moment she arrived, I became totally drunk. Did she drink a good dose of olive oil before making the trip to our evil den? Women could, at times, be a wonder and perhaps a little devious.

For the most part, it wasn't really a "den" of entrapment. We were young guys having spent too long a time at war, and we were looking forward to finding the right person to spend the rest of our lives with. I dare say the girls were doing the same. The war years had made both men and women hungry and happy for mutual companionship. So many of us had been deprived of a dating and social life during our years of what should have been normal romantic discovery, and we were now looking for a real and permanent connection. The men were handsome in their uniforms, the women lovely, and we were all desperately and, in many cases, perhaps hastily making up for lost time in seeking a life of love, starting a family, and happiness.

For the moment, though, flying was still paramount. Several Livermore episodes stand out in my memory. A new concept of instrument training was developed. Some of our Hellcats were outfitted with a lighttight surface on the inside of the canopy, permitting the pilot to undergo instrument training after he closed the canopy. For these training flights, a chase plane—another fighter—flew safety escort. The chase plane pilot's job was to keep airspace clear and advise the instrument pilot, who was executing a specific program, if he was becoming disoriented. Flying blind under controlled circumstances in the Hellcat helped prepare us for unexpected moments when vertigo became the enemy. It was a good learning experience.

Flight training wasn't always inner directed. A navy submarine was in position off the coast south of San Francisco, near Santa Cruz, and an exercise was scheduled for twelve fighters to rendezvous with the boat and make dummy runs on the sub so the sub's crew could practice surface gunnery, tracking us as though we were the enemy coming in on them. When we arrived on station at the scheduled hour, we circled with no sub in sight. They had been watching for us from periscope depth, and suddenly, the big dark hull of a rather prehistoric-looking sub emerged from the depths, water washing over her deck as sailors scrambled out of the conning tower and instantly manned the guns.

For me, this coordination of land and sea effort was a navy moment, instilling the same pride similar to marching down a street in Iowa City in the winter, singing "Anchors Aweigh." Flying just above the sea toward the ship was sheer fun—phantom runs, no real bullets flying, a battle at sea performed without casualties. It was straight out of a page of my imaginary drawings in my childhood school notebooks.

While we were enjoying ourselves, in reality, the weather had worsened. Low clouds hugged the coastal mountain range that separated the shoreline from Livermore, with an overcast bank hanging below the mountaintops. Circling, we could see the Link Observatory, with an elevation of 4,213 feet, on Mount Hamilton, which was just west of the beginning of the cloud cover.

Will's voice came over. "I think I remember a pass through the mountains to the valley. We'll go through, two planes at a time at three-minute intervals."

Buddy Bowen, a football player from Ole Miss and a complete Southern bon vivant, came on the air. "Will, I'd rather take my group up to San Francisco and follow the highway." Will agreed, and Bo headed north along the coast.

As part of Gove's group, we circled and checked watches as Will and his wingman entered the mountain tunnel. Continuing to circle, counting off the time, we entered the opening at our designated intervals. I took my wingman, a new guy relying on my experience, into the mountain channel of the unknown, keenly aware of my responsibility as his leader, his attention focused as he flew close formation on me.

I wasn't sure what to look for. With no defined route, the sides of all the mountains and terrain seemed to blend in with the ground below—no defined beginning or end. We were groping at 175 knots, and now there was no visible horizon. I can't recall if I was praying that we wouldn't fly into a mountain cul-de-sac. If I wasn't, I certainly should have been. Threading through the steep hills on either side, at times so narrow that, if we had to, we couldn't even have made a 180-degree turn, my mind kept zigzagging between escape and entrapment. After what seemed an endless route, the path opened up, and we soared into the valley; its wide-open space never looked so good. Upon landing at Livermore, we were met by Will Gove pacing the flight line, counting his chickens. We had all come home to safely roost once again.

The submarine assignment was brand new. Therefore, it was exciting and interesting to all of us. It wasn't in the fighter syllabus, which by now we had memorized.

In August 1944, while we were fighting in the Pacific, representatives from the United States, the Soviet Union, Great Britain, and China met outside Washington, DC, at Dumbarton Oaks, a handsome old Georgetown estate. At this meeting, called the Dumbarton Oaks Conference, the delegates agreed to form a new organization called the United Nations.

On April 25, 1945, men and women of forty-six nations gathered in San Francisco to draft a charter for the newly formed United Nations, and we had another one-of-a-kind nonsyllabus assignment. The delegates would be aboard the *Delta Queen,* a paddle wheel vessel used during peacetime to take passengers on excursions up the Sacramento River. The powers that be decided that all air groups in the Bay Area make a dummy "show" attack on the boat at a specified day and time as it toured San Francisco Bay. The navy was all set to show off its superb airpower.

On the appointed day, Air Group Thirteen rendezvoused over Livermore and headed for the bay at 8,000 feet. It was a grand idea, but unfortunately, there was no target coordinator as we arrived over the *Delta Queen.* We found ourselves among a lot of airplanes circling in no particular order, with some planes randomly diving toward the boat. Our division, spread out in loose formation, began its run. It immediately became apparent we were overtaking torpedo bombers and dive-bombers, all slower planes from another air group, in their dives. The sky became filled with planes in steep dives, converging on the United Nations passengers. If ever there was an air traffic controller's worst nightmare, this was it.

Passing bombers to our left, right, above, and below, we dived at the upturned faces gleaming in the California sun. Were they impressed? I'm sure they were. Were they frightened? I'm sure they were. I know I was. All the planes somehow managed to complete their runs without any midair collisions and returned to base—another miracle sent from above.

Nazi Reign Ends

- 72 -

Three and a half years after Pearl Harbor, the Allies had finally ended the German Nazi reign. City after city had been razed, killing many Germans and exposing the barbarity of National Socialism. Hitler had committed suicide.

May 8, 1945, was declared V-E Day, and President Truman dedicated the victory to former president Franklin D. Roosevelt, who had steered the nation through all the dark war years. It was sadly ironic that FDR died only a little over a month before of a cerebral hemorrhage, not living long enough to see the victory he had worked so hard to accomplish. There were celebrations across the country, especially in New York's Times Square, with sailors kissing nurses in the streets while news cameras flashed. It was a joyful roar for humanity—parades and flyovers took place, but the ebullience of V-E Day was not a conclusion to the war.

There were still thousands of Americans slugging it out, along with their families and loved ones back home, in the Pacific theater against the relentless Japanese. This part of the ongoing war was being fought in places with unfamiliar names, tiny island specks on a Pacific Ocean map. Where was Papua, Tuvalu, Balikpapan? Who ever heard of these places?

War bonds were still being sold to "help finish the job." America was tired and celebrating, but the war was still far from over. Veterans from the battlefields in Europe were being assembled on the West Coast, and plans were being made for an invasion of Japan that would dwarf the D-Day landings at Normandy. We were part of that plan.

In the midst of all their joy and jubilation, Americans forgot for the moment that the Japanese had not lost a war since 1591. This was their mindset. They were not going to give up.

V-J Day

- 73 -

We had completed the last stages of our stateside training before shipping out to Hawaii, where we were stationed at Barbers Point on Oahu—temporary headquarters. One of the first orders of business was our air combat intelligence officer's wedding in Honolulu. Scott McKeown was marrying a banker's daughter he had met in Honolulu on a previous assignment. My pals and I were invited. After the church wedding in Honolulu, the reception was held on the lawn of the banker's miniestate on Diamond Head. Champagne, champagne, and even more champagne flowed. It was quite a significant social event.

Marine captain Bob Crosby, brother of Bing, was there. (I used to listen to Crosby's Bob Cats before the war on a radio program broadcast from the Blackhawk in Chicago.) Duke Kahanamoku, the sheriff of Honolulu and former Olympic swimmer, was there, talking with Crosby along with other celebrities in attendance. I can't really name many famous names in attendance as Dorie, Higgins, Bowman, Pope, and I got too smashed on the excessive rounds of champagne. With champagne-induced singing, we merrily left the party and walked down the middle of the street, heading for a navy bus back to the base.

In August, the squadron conducted day carrier requalification exercises aboard the USS *Saratoga*. On the first day of these exercises, Air Group Thirteen broke the fleet record for carrier landing aboard a carrier in one day, completing 634 landings in ten hours.

Somewhere in his early navy experience, Fred Griffen—VF-13's "acquisition officer" and Boston native—met Johnny Pesky, a player on the Boston Red Sox who enlisted in the navy. Griff was one of those guys who became everyone's friend after their first handshake. While we were at Maui, awaiting fleet orders, there was an all-service baseball World Series being held on Oahu. Pesky was playing. Ever the promoter, Griff determined that he, Higgins, Dorie, and I assign ourselves four Hellcats and fly to Oahu to meet Johnny and watch a game, which we did, meeting him after the game at the BOQ on Ford Island.

Pesky played shortstop and had one hell of a rifle throw. I shook hands with him and was surprised at the looseness of his right arm. It seemed as though I was shaking his hand right up to his shoulder. It's hard to describe the feeling of his flexibility—it was surprising and almost nonathletic. We made several flights from Puunene to watch the series. I was never a big fan of baseball, but I did enjoy meeting Johnny and watching him use that powerful, flexible arm.

While we were readying to return to the Pacific battle, America's new B-29 bombers had been dropping incendiaries on one Japanese city after another, igniting storms of fire that burned thousands of men, women, and children in a hellscape of death. In spite of the maelstroms of fire, the Japanese rejected the Potsdam Declaration's attempt to end the war and refused to surrender. We were stationed at Barbers Point when, on August 6, 1945, the atomic bomb was dropped on Hiroshima. In the blink of an eye, the city was reduced to molten glass and ash, and thousands of inhabitants simply vanished. Despite this brutal massive destruction and an enormous loss of lives, the Japanese still refused to surrender; and as a reaction, on August 9, a second bomb was dropped and annihilated the city of Nagasaki.

On August 15, 1945, V-J Day, Japan finally surrendered with a formal signing on September 2, taking place aboard the US battleship

Missouri. The war in the Pacific had finally come to an end. Did we ever celebrate! The ground floor of the huge Quonset hut we were housed in was awash with water from molten ice cubes and bourbon. We were as jubilant as if a major holiday had been declared. The war was finally over.

Or Was It?

- 74 -

The war on the European front was definitely over, but there were those who still did not trust the Japanese. The elation we felt when it seemed as though the war was over on both fronts was tempered by uncertainty. We wanted to celebrate—we were eager to return to the United States, yet anxiety hung like a pall, mocking our celebration.

Scuttlebutt said the navy wasn't positive that the war was indeed over. Had the Japanese really given up, or was this just a silent pause due to their fear of a new Russian threat on their other front? Suspicious of the Japanese and concerned that this might be yet another ruse, naval leaders strove to keep the navy's air and sea muscle firm. They were not yet ready to relax their well-oiled fighting machine.

Thus followed unsettled days when the atmosphere among the squadron was one of anticipation seasoned by rumor. The navy regrouped, and we set up flight operations, first at NAS Puunene and then NAS Kahului, Maui. The brass was uneasy. We proceeded to continue syllabus training, readying ourselves for a night carrier landing checkout session aboard the USS *Corregidor*, only a month after the big truce-signing event on the battleship *Missouri* in Tokyo Bay.

As part of that preparation, the air group spent two days aboard the USS *Saratoga*, where on the first day of these exercises Air Group

Thirteen broke another fleet record for carrier landings in one day, completing 643 landings in ten hours. During this period, we were fully engaged in routine training flights and ground training. While we were not engaged in action with the enemy, the training was still intensive and still subject to simple human error.

After taking off from Puunene one afternoon, our division flew into the crater of Mount Haleakala, the extinct volcano on Maui. We were on our way to field carrier landing and night carrier landing practice on a fighter strip at Upolu Point on the edge of Kailua Bay on the Big Island, Hawaii. On the north side of the crater was a large break where, many years ago, the lava collapsed the rim of the volcano and cascaded down to the ocean, ten thousand feet below.

With enough room for us to fly through and in formation, we dived toward the ocean floor, following the contour of the mountain as though we were on a giant 250-knot toboggan ride. Halfway down, one of the sections of my engine cowling that held it in place left the cowling banging in the wind, threatening to fly off. I pulled out of the dive, reduced speed, and headed back to Kahului, where I landed, wondering if our mechanics had decided their war was over and they could slack off—the plane was supposed to have had an engine check the night before. Had the cowling broken loose, it would have wiped off the canopy, the housing that surrounded my head and shoulders, not to mention me. That was the first of three of what I'd call slacking-off incidents.

The second incident also occurred when our division was headed for the fighter strip on Upolu Point. Four of us were flying just above the blue Hawaiian waters when I thought I detected a burp in the engine—a slight miss. Then there were several more hiccups, almost imperceptible, so I wasn't overconcerned.

We arrived over the strip and broke off into the landing pattern for a series of late afternoon field carrier landings practice before dinner and night practice, touch-and-go landings. I came around into the groove for my first approach, got a cut, and applied full power, and the engine quit. It just stopped, no power at all, nada, with the propeller slowly winding down as the plane rolled down the runway. I applied the brakes and turned off on a taxi strip where the plane rolled to a stop, and I waited for transportation. It reminded me a little of my dead stick landing way back at Kingsville.

During dinner, Chief Petty Officer Galka—our head guy in charge of aircraft maintenance—informed me that a butterfly valve had stuck, and the problem was taken care of. My engine and I made the next required number of landings in the middle of the night without any more burps. Fortunately, there were no accidents or incidents aboard the *Corregidor*, and everyone came through the night landing qualifications unscathed.

We were not a happy group. We were tired, relieved that the war was over, yet we entertained the nagging fear of not being assured it was. It was like having one foot on the dock and one on the boat.

Incident number three was a little more serious. It was early October 1945, and the navy was going to put on an air show for civilians on the twenty-seventh—Navy Day. They wanted a few tail chases, some low-level attacks on the field, maybe a field carrier landing demonstration—the usual air show-off stuff. Sixteen planes were scheduled for tail chase practice, a routine all of us had participated in innumerable times during training and as a squadron.

We climbed to altitude over Kahului Bay, about ten thousand feet, and formed up, line astern. The leader—our skipper, Ace King—began a long steep dive before pulling into a loop. I was near the end of the line, a nasty position because you were doomed to fly through the prop wash of all the planes ahead of you, which caused your plane to whip from side to side in the turbulent air. It wasn't unusual for your head to bang against the side of the canopy.

On the way down, doing about 350 knots before pull-up, my canopy started rattling on the port side. The speed with which things happened, and therefore the surprise, is difficult to describe. The canopy came off its track, caught in the wind, and crunched down on my head like a heavy metal bag. The blow didn't knock me out. It crushed down just far enough so that I could still sink lower into my seat. I pulled up, level, and away from the group and headed for the field. The blow split the skin on my scalp, the blood giving me an unfashionable red rinse.

Years later, when fiberglass helmets were introduced and the days of cloth helmets and silk scarves were history, I remembered what a good idea that protection would have been at the time.

I was concentrating so hard on landing safely that I didn't realize my wingman, George Edmonson, was flying with me, escorting me to safety. I became angry with the traffic controllers in the tower. I had declared my emergency but had to delay landing because another plane on final continued while he should have been told to go around. During a later phone call, they said they didn't have radio contact with that plane. I wondered if they had ever heard of using an Aldis lamp to wave off planes. It seemed as though almost everyone was relaxing.

I landed and taxied to the fighter ramp, where my pals pulled the canopy open and helped me out of the cockpit and out of my Mae West and helmet, both soaked with blood, as was my shirt. The base hospital was on the other side of the field. Had I known that, I could have taxied to that side, or the tower could have directed me if they were on the stick.

An ammunition truck—an open, flatbed vehicle, sturdy and muscular, acting as an ambulance—was quickly provided. I sat in the back on top of an empty ammo box, hanging on for dear life. The driver, seeing all the blood (head injuries are famous for that), assumed that it was life and death and drove accordingly, circling the field at full speed and swerving off the road into the gravel several times. Given the looks on the faces of the two enlisted men in the truck, I was starting to get pretty scared myself.

We made it in one piece, and the air group flight surgeon, Doc Reid, hustled me into a treatment room, washed the wound, shaved the area, and tried to close it with butterfly clamps, which slid right off. He then resorted to stitches instead and doused my head with what must have been a pound of sulfa powder and proceeded to create a white turban for me. Thus ended incident number three.

All hands were beginning to show a letdown mode; call it dog tired and perhaps worn out if you will. The squadron was falling apart—even though new people were assigned, the core spirit that had seen Fighting Thirteen through tough times and sad moments was gone.

Our planes, always perfectly maintained, began to demonstrate flaws. I knew that this was still a very dangerous game we were playing, but now in my mind, it seemed more of a game than serious battle training.

Finally, word came from the brass above with orders to decommission Air Group Thirteen. During a quiet small ceremony at Kahului, I attended in my doctor's designer white head turban while Commander Kibbe, now air group commander, formally reviewed the assembled officers and enlisted men. He stopped his brisk walk in front of me and, smiling, said, "How are you feeling, son?"

Eventually, my sheikh turban went into the trash, the sulfa came off in chunks, and my stitches were pulled out. I had a three-inch scar to tell the tale. Life went on.

Part Seven
Postwar

Finally home
933 Monica Ave, Detroit Michigan

It's Really Over

- 75 -

The navy finally admitted the war was over. After our squadron was decommissioned, we sat around feeling like people without a country, waiting to be sent where? There was a discharge point system divided into two parts—married and unmarried personnel. It was based on one's length of service, age, and rank. Either the married guys were already gone or their bags were packed. Gove and Sullivan, among them, were returned to the States. The navy was wondering what to do with all their unmarried studs who hadn't quite yet reached discharge time now that we didn't have planes to shoot at.

They decided we would be excellent recruits to help man troopships, the small carriers used for evacuating thousands of the military from the Pacific theatre. Welders were working overtime, fastening racks to steel bulkheads to provide sleeping space. We could volunteer for this duty if we chose.

Gene Higgins, Jim Nickoloff, and I were eager to head for Japan instead. Aerial war had been dispassionate—we fought and shot airplanes, not people. Our mental and physical energy had been focused on Japan for years, and we thought that perhaps by going to Japan, our aggression might be sated. It seemed anticlimactic not to reach the target country, so the three of us signed up. There was one slight emotional status problem—aviators always wore brown shoes with their tan and green uniforms. Becoming part of a ship's company, we would now have to become one of the black-shoe crowd. Could we stand wearing black shoes? Much to our relief, we learned we wouldn't suffer our loss of status—we wouldn't have to give up our brown shoes.

With the point system, we wouldn't be eligible for discharge for another six months, so we waited, methodically checking each day to see if our ship assignment was posted. After three weeks of total boredom, our names were finally listed. We were to report to the executive officer of the USS *Attu*—a small carrier. We were finally on our way to Japan.

As required, we went aboard and presented ourselves and our orders. When the exec looked at our point status, he grimaced and said, "By the time we train you for your duties aboard, you'll be eligible for discharge. I'll sign your papers now. You'll be discharged when we reach Long Beach." The ship, loaded with troops, was bound for Long Beach, California. *So long, Tokyo. We'll never get to see you. And hello, California, once again.*

Instead of being discharged at San Diego, as we thought we would be, I was sent to Glenview, Illinois, to be released, and Gene was sent to New York City. Nickoloff was from Los Angeles, so he was already home. My discharge procedure was executed at Glenview, and I bought a train ticket from Chicago to Detroit. Once aboard with some precious quiet time to myself, I sat and reflected on the past few years.

I had finally fulfilled my childhood dream of flying. All of us had been just boys when we enlisted, right on the cusp of manhood, young men testing the mettle of our convictions who were forced to grow up quickly. We had seen our young friends die who would never fulfill their dreams. At the same time, I also had the honor and privilege of being part of an air group that was a remarkable organization. I thought of how fortunate I was to have been in the company of the Fighting Squadron Thirteen, a proud small band of warriors who dedicated their lives to their country, along with the millions of other men and women who stepped forward, whether on land, air, or sea, in one joint effort. And yes, I had also been unlucky and heartbroken at love.

I realized as the train swayed back and forth, heading home, that an entire chapter of my life was now coming to a close, and I wondered what the future would hold. There would be a whole new adventure ahead of me, new goals and challenges with unknown chapters to be written. My mind kept jumping between luck and God. I liked to think he had a lot to do with my survival, and I attributed him to having his hand on the stick when I was upside down over Salton Sea and being shot at in the air, but I also never lost faith in my luck as well. I kept luck in a pocket of my flight suit, and it had come in handy.

The train finally pulled into the station that hot August evening. I took a cab from the station to 9333 Monica Ave., paid the driver, hauled my two pieces of navy luggage up the front steps, and stopped to look into the front bay window. My mom and dad were sitting in the living room, quietly reading the *Detroit News*. I hadn't phoned ahead. This would be the surprise of their lives. I rang the doorbell.

Fighting Squadron Thirteen Reunion

1984

In 1984, when notified of the squadron's second reunion, which was to be held in Pensacola, Florida, I resisted the idea as I had the first reunion. I've always disliked going back in time and place. The same negative forces were now at work. I had emotional difficulty making a decision to attend. Frankly, I just didn't want to go.

The dichotomy is I've written about the past and about the squadron and assorted flying experiences with enthusiasm, dedication, affection, and love for my squadron buddies, fully recognizing the significance of that stretch of my life. Earning my navy wings of gold defined me as a person—a boy who became a man. I emerged from cadet to officer to a fighter aviator who, yes, took lives defending our country. We came away from all that with the memory of our luck, what we had seen, and I suppose all of us tried not to wonder too much how we managed to survive and others didn't.

I don't know what changed my mind. Perhaps it was the persuasiveness of my buddies Gene Higgins and Bill Dorie. Most likely, it was my wife, Nancy. Never one to mince words, she simply said, "Go. If you don't, you'll regret it." With that command, off I went.

Once there, I was overwhelmed by the spirit of the event and the joy of seeing all my friends again. The hotel was on the Gulf of Mexico, which had a large tiki hut, on the white sand beach where we had a rousing party the first evening. There were two reunion highlights.

One was the surprise appearance of a voluptuous blonde in a full mermaid costume whose appearance was arranged by Ozzy Osborne, chairman of the gala. Cameras flashed, and wives snickered while the young woman was having as much fun as we were. The evening took me back to our simple ready room parties so many years ago when our young spirits soared—now we were much older graying spirits but still soaring.

The second highlight was the squadron dinner held on the last evening of the reunion at the NAS Pensacola officer's club. It was a more formal evening where we wore sport coats and ties, a change from the leisure khakis and sport shirts on "mermaid night." After the cocktail hour, we sat at large round tables, and Johnny Langford stood at the dais and began a remarkable story.

He had recently attended a religious retreat where he met a man from Windsor, Connecticut. This man had been carrying a pilot's log with him for years, expecting, hoping one day he would somehow meet one of the pilot's squadron mates from WWII. He wanted to be sure they would receive the written personal account of the flier's experiences in 1944. Johnny then read Lt. (j.g.) Robert Brooks's combat journal to the silent and very attentive audience.

LEYTE: DULAG FIELD THREE DAYS LATER

WRITTEN BY LT. JIM POPE

I gave this log (Foregoing accounts written by Bobby Brooks in his own hand writing, every nite upon his return from his mission—condensed in these pages from 45 combat missions) to Donald S. Smith of Ridgewood Road, officer on the same carrier with Bobby Brooks to give to you (Mrs. Brooks, Bobby's mother). We were not established on the Island of Leyte with our US Forces, where Bobby's last mission took place. You will find DULAG on the map, on the East Coast of the Island about a mile inland. DULAG FIELD is where we had to land that night and as the field had been in US hands only two days, the field was only under construction. Bobby could not bail out over the field because the enemy lines were too close. Bobby was not excited the least bit. He was exactly the opposite. His making a landing on the field, he knew was impossible as his plane was damaged, the wheels were pretty well shot up early in the flight, when we encountered Zeros. Bobby himself shot down one of them. When he could not land on the field, he did the only thing left to do, went toward the wind, for altitude, to bail out and float back to DULAG. Unfortunately it was growing dark, night was coming on. The last we heard, he was ready to bail out. This ends the Log Record of Bobby Brooks.

We were all silent for quite a while, remembering someone who had made the ultimate sacrifice for our country. It was then I knew why I shouldn't have missed this reunion. Brooksie was there.

"We recreated our 'buddy' photo when we met at
the reunion — older, wiser but still spry."

A Tribute

A friend once asked me if I had any guilt about being a survivor. The thought had never occurred to me. It made me think, however, which may have been what the question was intended to do.

It took me into deep crevices of sadness, remembering, wondering, questioning, searching for logic that had always defied reason. I thought about my friends who would never have children. I thought about the wives and children left alone. But I had no guilty feelings about being a survivor. I was simply lucky. Friends say it was God's will I survived. Over the course of a lifetime, I have sought explanations but found none.

Perhaps the most frightening part of war was that death was so random. Many of my friends died. I didn't.

The rationale I developed—and I believe, we all had built some sort of mental armor, or call it denial—was that my friends didn't die. They just flew to some unknown island. Perhaps they're there waiting for me.

Ad Mare—Ad Astra

(Toward the Sea—Toward the Stars)
No shallow tribute
Marked on graven stone
Commemorates their dust—
Rather, their grave
Is as deep and vast and enduring
As the love in the hearts of strong men.

———————————————————————————————
——————————————

Lt. (j.g.) Frederick Beckman
Lt. (j.g.) Joseph Kopman
Lt. Clarence "Kelly" Blair
Lt. (j.g.) Richard Bridge
Ensign Roger L'Estrange
Lt. Eric Magnusson
Lt. (j.g.) Robert Brooks
Ensign Robert Martin
Ensign Norman Drouin
Ensign Paul Parent
Ensign Joseph Heinrich
Ensign Benjamin Miles
Lt. Wade Winecoff

Lt. Ancil "Ted" Hudson
Lt. (j.g.) Warren E. Wolfe
Ensign Christopher Gibbs

———————————————————————————————————

——————————————————

Ensign Nikolay Liszak Ensign Paul Spendley

———————————————————————————————————

——————————————————

Ensign John Carroll's PBM patrol plane went down in a storm off the coast of South America. All hands were lost.

———————————————————————————————————

——————————————————

Lt. Edward Armstrong, my fraternity brother, was killed when his Airacobra fighter crashed during a training flight.

———————————————————————————————————

——————————————————

At 1215 on July 30, 1945, while on her way from Guam to Okinawa, unescorted, the heavy cruiser USS *Indianapolis* was struck by two Japanese torpedoes and sank. Three hundred sixteen men were saved; 883 died. My freshman English teacher Lt. Theodore Miles was one of the 883.

Epilogue

Final Entry In Bob's Journal

A Love Letter to Bob
From Nancy
July 20, 2020

The dementia set in like a menacing gray fog quietly, slowly seeping into the tiny corners of his mind, almost silent and sneaky at first. Its cloudiness began to confuse names and dates, and then it began to form a thicker blanket that continued to creep until it started confusing the way to the store, my birthday, his grandchildren's names.

Anger, frustration, and embarrassment became like an uninvited guest, so we would pretend it was not unlike the heavy cloud banks he had encountered and flown through as an aviator. "It isn't the first thick cloud bank you've flown through," I assured him. Sometimes there were kind breaks in the clouds when the sun would shine through for periods, each sunny moment becoming a treasured gift.

We had dinner every evening in sync with the six o'clock news, which was also often the most picturesque time of the day for us—the sun setting in the west, usually turning into a spectacular ball of fire while slowly sinking down into the dark blue waters of the bay, all of which we were fortunate enough to view from our cottage window.

We would critique the almost magical vivid colors that would intensify and then produce a magnificent afterglow of yellows, pinks, and rosy reds, outlining every silver and gray cloud, always leaving us in awe of how wonderful life and nature was.

But as the fog continued to thicken within his brain, sunset also meant a time of increased confusion, frustration, and agitation, also known as sundown syndrome, a symptom that is part of midstage to advanced dementia. I never knew what the magnificent sunset would bring—joy, anger, fear, or wandering. Thought to be triggered by fading light, it was almost a cruel irony that such beauty could bring on symptoms that would become worse as the night went on and then, as though by magic, evaporates with the morning light.

He fought hard to fly through this fog in the past sixteen years, some days with success, other days with difficulty but not without a sense of humor, which he never lost. "Nancy, this is important," he said on one such evening. "I haven't called my dad. I need to check on how he's doing." He stopped his dinner with a concerned voice.

I sighed and quietly replied that his dad had been gone for many, many years now.

He looked at me, half-believing me yet half not.

I continued, "Figure it out, sweetie. How old are you?"

He was not sure, and he hated it when he became caught with the cruel confusion of time, names, and dates.

So I told him, "You were ninety-eight last November."

"I am?" Now there was a long pause, and I can see the wheels spinning. He resumed eating his dinner and muttered, "That's pretty damn old."

Bob just wouldn't eat his dinner and only picked at breakfast. Forget about lunch—that time had become relegated to nap time. I said, "Bob, remember the last doctor we saw a long time ago when you wouldn't eat?"

He stared at me with his newly acquired sheepish look while twisting and examining his fingers and said, "I think so."

"Then repeat it," I said in my schoolteacher voice, which had not been serving me well the past few weeks.

"If you don't eat, you die," he replied with a half smile, testing my reaction.

"You got it 100 percent right, sweetie," I replied, tears starting to well up. "So let's try to remember that, OK?"

He nodded, saying, "I'll try harder."

July 2

Oatmeal breakfast—his favorite apple and cinnamon loaded with Boost instead of milk. The new aide is sitting at the table with us, and I have the computer open, working on "our book."

"Bob," I say, "do you remember what the name of the pavilion was where you took Mary, your sweetheart, dancing in Detroit way back in the '20s? I can't remember the name." I am planting a fake memory test question.

He stares at his oatmeal for about two minutes and looks up with a smile and says, "The Bob-O where all the big bands like Dorsey played. Boy, did we love to dance!"

"Right, I couldn't remember!" I exclaim and look at the aide as we both smile at each other.

In the middle of watching the evening news, Bob asks, "Do you believe there's a heaven?" This one comes at me out of the blue. He doesn't speak about death at all.

I answer, "Yes, I do believe. I'm not sure I buy into the gateways and fluffy clouds, but I am sure that we will all receive peace from a loving God who is far beyond our understanding."

I see him pondering this one, and I want to make him smile. "Just remember what our friend Dale always said. 'When you get up there, turn right. Don't make a left.' Then you have to look for Doug because I'm sure he'll have an ice-cold martini ready. And my *tante* is always game for a drink and a round of poker."

He starts to laugh at this one. I just love seeing him laugh.

July 3

I'm on the computer while Bob is eating his oatmeal. He asks, "What are you doing?"

"I'm working on our book," I reply. I explain that it's just about ready for a final read and some tweaking.

He's quiet and asks, "Do you think it's any good?"

I tell him that I think it's a tender story of an idealistic young man who romanticizes going to war, sets high goals, and accomplishes all of them. "It's about you."

He's quiet again and says, "It's taken such a long time, Nancy."

I tell him it was too good to rush and that we both spent lots of time working on it, which was kind of fun. He nods and I tear up again, noticing how frail he has become. I know he's putting on a brave front to please me.

The book, our book, has become like the O'Henry story "The Last Leaf." Each time he starts to fade or sink, I remind him he's not going anywhere. The book isn't done yet.

July 4

I hold his hand during his labored breathing, and he whispers, "I think I'm dying, Nancy."

I squeeze his hand and whisper, "I'm right here with you, helping you get ready for your new flight." Then I give him a dab of the medication on his tongue that will ease his anxiety and labored breathing, and he drifts off.

July 5

I give him sips of water and sponge him off, wetting his lips and mouth. He's now in the "land of takeoff," just about ready to leave me. I hold his hand on and off all day until his labored breathing stops at 9:45 p.m.

"So long, ace," I whisper as I kiss him goodbye. "I love you. Fly high."

"Fair Winds and Following Seas"

"Aviation gave me structure — Sailing in
wind, clean and free, gave me peace".
November 7, 1921—July 5, 2020
"Well Done"